A COMMUNICATIVE APPROACH TO THE TOEIC® L&R TEST
Book 3: Advanced

Teruhiko Kadoyama
Simon Capper

 SEIBIDO

photographs by
iStockphoto

音声ファイルのダウンロード／ストリーミング

CD マーク表示がある箇所は、音声を弊社 HP より無料でダウンロード／ストリーミングすることができます。下記 URL の書籍詳細ページに音声ダウンロードアイコンがございますのでそちらから自習用音声としてご活用ください。

https://www.seibido.co.jp/ad695

A COMMUNICATIVE APPROACH TO THE TOEIC® L&R TEST
Book 3: Advanced

LINGUAPORTA

リンガポルタのご案内

> **リンガポルタ連動テキストをご購入の学生さんは、「リンガポルタ」を無料でご利用いただけます！**

　本テキストで学習していただく内容に準拠した問題を、オンライン学習システム「リンガポルタ」で学習していただくことができます。PCだけでなく、スマートフォンやタブレットでも学習できます。単語や文法、リスニング力などをよりしっかり身に付けていただくため、ぜひ積極的に活用してください。

　リンガポルタの利用にはアカウントとアクセスコードの登録が必要です。登録方法については下記ページにアクセスしてください。

https://www.seibido.co.jp/linguaporta/register.html

本テキスト「A COMMUNICATIVE APPROACH TO THE TOEIC® L&R TEST Book 3: Advanced」のアクセスコードは下記です。

7291-2048-1231-0365-0003-0076-Q4HJ-BL4X

・リンガポルタの学習機能（画像はサンプルです。また、すべてのテキストに以下の4つの機能が用意されているわけではありません）

● 多肢選択

● 空所補充（音声を使っての聞き取り問題も可能）

● 単語並びかえ（マウスや手で単語を移動）

● マッチング（マウスや手で単語を移動）

complain	（労力・時間・金など）を節約する
celebrate	（こと）を制限・限定する
restrict	満足させる
save	〜を祝う
satisfy	不平（不満・文句）を言う

は し が き

　本書は、A Communicative Approach to the TOEIC® L&R Test シリーズの上級編であり、主に TOEIC® Listening and Reading Test（以下、TOEIC L&R テスト）でスコア 600 以上を目指す方を対象としています。TOEIC L&R テスト対策のテキストは数多く出版されていますが、本書の特徴は、タイトルが示すように、コミュニケーションに焦点を当てたアプローチを採用した試験対策テキストであるという点です。具体的には、実践形式で練習問題を解いた後、問題で使われた対話や文書を活用して、パートナーと互いに英語で質問したり、質問に答えたりするコミュニケーション演習が本書には豊富に含まれています。試験対策の授業では予想問題を解くのが中心で、英語を話す機会がほとんどない場合もありますが、このテキストで学習することにより、単に TOEIC L&R テストのスコアアップだけではなく、英語のコミュニケーション能力を向上させることも可能となるでしょう。

　この他にも本書には次のような特徴があります。

　まず、各ユニットの最初にある Vocabulary のセクションでは、語彙の中でも特に派生語の増強に焦点を当てています。Part 5 の文法問題では正しい品詞を選ぶ問題が数多く出題されますが、派生語の知識を増やすことで、未知の単語であっても、語尾から意味や品詞を推測できるようになるでしょう。

　次に、各パートの問題を解くうえで知っておくべき重要項目を「解法のコツ」としてまとめており、効率的な学習が可能です。Part 3〜4 の図表問題や Part 6 の文挿入問題など、TOEIC L&R テストには特徴的な設問がいろいろありますが、解法のコツをマスターすることでそれらにも十分対応できるはずです。

　この他にも、本書は Web 英語学習システムの LINGUAPORTA（リンガポルタ）に対応していますので、パソコンやスマートフォンを使ったモバイル・ラーニングが可能です。

　TOEIC L&R テストは約 2 時間で200問の問題を解かなければならず、スコアアップを図るにはやはり地道な英語学習が必要とされます。本書での学習が、皆さんの目標スコア獲得や英語コミュニケーション能力の涵養に役立てば、筆者としてこれ以上の喜びはありません。

　また、本書の刊行にあたっては、成美堂の佐野英一郎社長、そして編集部の工藤隆志氏、萩原美奈子氏に多大なご尽力を賜りました。衷心よりお礼申し上げます。

角山照彦
Simon Capper

Table of Contents

本書の構成と使い方

本書は、オフィス、ショッピング、レストランなど、TOEIC L&R テストに頻出のテーマを取り上げた全 14 ユニットで構成されています。また、各ユニットは次のような構成になっています。

名詞・動詞・形容詞・副詞を作る接尾辞を取り上げ、未知の単語を見た際に品詞や意味が推測できるよう、派生語の知識を増やします。

Vocabulary

TOEIC L&R テスト対策で重要となる語彙力アップのための演習問題を用意しています。

ユニットのテーマに関する語彙を学習します。

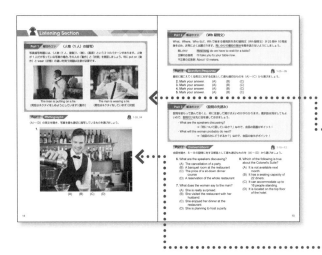

Listening Section

Part 1〜4 について、解法のコツと演習問題を用意しています。

頻出問題の解き方など、各パートの問題を解く際に必要な解法のコツを学習します。

解法のコツ で取り上げた内容を含む演習問題に取り組むことで実践力アップを目指します。

Communicative Training (Listening Section)

Part 2〜3 で取り上げた応答や対話を使ってパートナーと互いに英語で質問をしたり、質問に答えたりする演習です。

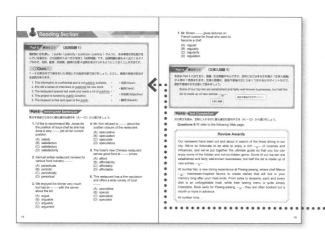

Reading Section

Part 5~7 について、解法のコツと
演習問題を用意しています。

頻出問題の解き方など、各パー
トの問題を解く際に必要な解法
のコツを学習します。

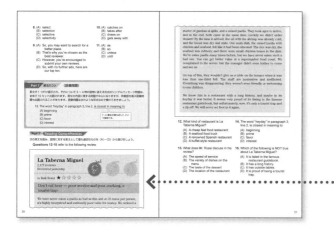

解法のコツ で取り上げた内容
を含む演習問題に取り組むこと
で実践力アップを目指します。

Communicative Training
(Reading Section)

Part 7 で取り上げた文書を
使ってパートナーと互いに英語
で質問をしたり、質問に答えた
りする演習です。

TOEIC® Listening and Reading Test について

　TOEIC® Listening and Reading Test（以下、TOEIC L&R テスト）は、アメリカの非営利団体 Educational Testing Service（ETS）によって開発されたテストです。TOEIC とは、**T**est **O**f **E**nglish for **I**nternational **C**ommunication の略称で、オフィスや日常生活における英語コミュニケーション能力を幅広く測定するテストですが、TOEIC L&R テストは、その中でも特に Listening と Reading の能力を測定するものです。（TOEIC テストには、TOEIC L&R テストの他にも TOEIC® Speaking & Writing Tests や TOEIC® Speaking Test があります。）

評価方法

　TOEIC L&R テストの結果は、合格や不合格ではなく、10 点から 990 点までのスコアで評価されます（リスニングセクション：5〜495 点、リーディングセクション：5〜495 点）。トータルスコアの基準は常に一定であり、英語能力に変化がない限りスコアも一定に保たれます。

問題形式

　リスニングセクション（約 45 分間・100問）とリーディングセクション（75 分間・100問）から構成されおり、約 2 時間で 200問の問題に解答しなければなりません。各セクションは、次の表が示すように、7 つのパートに分かれています。

セクション	パート	名称		形式	問題数
リスニングセクション	1	Photographs	写真描写問題	4 択	6 問
	2	Question-Response	応答問題	3 択	25 問
	3	Conversations	会話問題	4 択	39 問
	4	Talks	説明文問題	4 択	30 問
リーディングセクション	5	Incomplete Sentences	短文穴埋め問題	4 択	30 問
	6	Text Completion	長文穴埋め問題	4 択	16 問
	7	Reading Comprehension	読解問題	4 択	54 問

また、各パートの形式は以下のとおりです。

Part 1 Photographs

1枚の写真について4つの短い説明文が1度だけ放送され、4つのうち写真を最も適切に描写しているものを選ぶ問題です。問題用紙には右のような写真のみで、説明文は印刷されていません。実際のテストでは6問出題され、解答時間は1問あたり約5秒です。

【問題例】

1.

Part 2 Question-Response

1つの質問（または発言）と、3つの応答がそれぞれ1度だけ放送され、質問に対して最も適切な応答を3つの中から選ぶ問題です。問題用紙には質問も応答も印刷されていません。実際のテストでは25問出題され、解答時間は1問あたり約5秒です。

【問題例】

7. Mark your answer on your answer sheet.

Part 3 Conversations

会話が1度だけ放送され、その後に設問が続きます。会話は印刷されていません。問題用紙の設問と4つの選択肢を読み、その中から最も適切なものを選ぶ問題です。実際のテストでは39問出題されます。解答時間は1問あたり約8秒ですが、図表問題のみ約12秒となっています。

【問題例】

32. Where does the woman work?

(A) At a restaurant
(B) At a hospital
(C) At a school
(D) At a post office

Part 4 Talks

アナウンスや電話のメッセージなどの説明文（トーク）が1度だけ放送され、その後に設問が続きます。説明文は印刷されていません。問題用紙の設問と4つの選択肢を読み、その中から最も適切なものを選ぶ問題です。実際のテストでは30問出題されます。解答時間は1問あたり約8秒ですが、図表問題のみ約12秒となっています。

【問題例】

71. What is being advertised?

(A) A pharmacy
(B) A movie theater
(C) A fitness center
(D) A supermarket

Part 5 ▸ Incomplete Sentences

4つの選択肢の中から最も適切なものを選び、不完全な文を完成させる問題です。実際のテストでは30問出題されます。

【問題例】

101. Oysters are a ------- of this restaurant.

(A) special
(B) specialize
(C) specially
(D) specialty

Part 6 ▸ Text Completion

4つの選択肢の中から最も適切なものを選び、不完全な文書を完成させる問題です。実際のテストでは、1つの長文に対して4問ずつ問題があり、合計16問出題されます。

【問題例】

Online shopping is a fast-growing market in the U.S. In a survey ------- in May last year, 40 percent of U.S.-based Internet users answered that they bought goods online several times a month.
131.

131. (A) conduct
(B) conducting
(C) conducted
(D) conducts

Part 7 ▸ Reading Comprehension

様々な形式の文書が提示され、それに関する設問と4つの選択肢を読んでその中から最も適切なものを選ぶ問題です。実際のテストでは、1つの文書に関する問題（シングルパッセージ問題）が29問、複数の文書に関する問題（ダブルパッセージ問題・トリプルパッセージ問題）が25問出題されます。

【問題例】

Dear all,
I hope this e-mail finds you all well.

147. The word "recommend" in paragraph 1, line 7, is closest in meaning to

(A) suggest
(B) deliver
(C) provide
(D) avoid

UNIT 01 Restaurants

ABCD Vocabulary

1. 1 〜 10 の語句の意味として適切なものを a 〜 j の中から選びましょう。 🎧 1-02

1. flavor	＿＿＿	a ．	バイキング（セルフサービス）形式の食事
2. anniversary	＿＿＿	b ．	料理、食事
3. banquet	＿＿＿	c ．	収容可能人数
4. server	＿＿＿	d ．	菜食主義者
5. vegetarian	＿＿＿	e ．	給仕人、接客係
6. ultimate	＿＿＿	f ．	（格別の）楽しみ、ごちそう
7. buffet	＿＿＿	g ．	記念日、〜周年
8. capacity	＿＿＿	h ．	（食べ物の）風味、香辛料
9. treat	＿＿＿	i ．	究極の、最高の
10. cuisine	＿＿＿	j ．	宴会、晩餐会

2. 語群の中から適切な日本語訳を選び、派生語の図を完成させましょう。

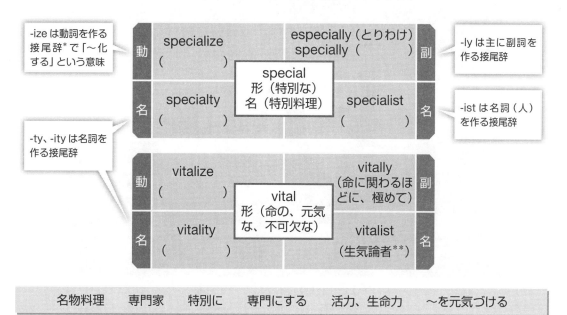

-ize は動詞を作る接尾辞*で「〜化する」という意味

動 specialize
（　　　　　）

especially（とりわけ）
specially（　　　）副

special
形（特別な）
名（特別料理）

-ly は主に副詞を作る接尾辞

名 specialty
（　　　　　）

specialist
（　　　　　）名

-ist は名詞（人）を作る接尾辞

-ty、-ity は名詞を作る接尾辞

動 vitalize
（　　　　　）

vitally
（命に関わるほどに、極めて）副

vital
形（命の、元気な、不可欠な）

名 vitality
（　　　　　）

vitalist
（生気論者**）名

名物料理	専門家	特別に	専門にする	活力、生命力	〜を元気づける

Note

*接尾辞とは、specialist の -ist など、語の後ろに付けられる要素を指します。接尾辞を付けることにより品詞が変化することが多く、接尾辞を見ると品詞が推測できます。
**生気論（せいきろん、vitalism）は、「生命に非生物にはない特別な力を認める」とする学問のことです。

13

Listening Section

Part 1	解法のコツ	〈人物（1人）の描写〉

写真描写問題には、〈人物（1人、複数）〉、〈物〉、〈風景〉という3つのパターンがあります。人物が1人だけ写っている写真の場合、その人の「動作」と「状態」を確認しましょう。特にput on（動作）とwear（状態）の違いを問う問題は注意が必要です。

The man is putting on a tie.
（男性はネクタイをしめようとしています）[動作]

The man is wearing a tie.
（男性はネクタイをしています）[状態]

Part 1	Photographs

🎧 1-03, 04

(A)〜(D) の英文を聞き、写真を最も適切に描写しているものを選びましょう。

1.

(A)　　(B)　　(C)　　(D)

Part 2 解法のコツ 〈Wh 疑問文〉

What、Where、Who など、Wh で始まる疑問詞を含む疑問文（Wh 疑問文）が 25 問中 10 問前後を占め、非常によく出題されます。問いかけの最初の部分を聞き逃さないようにしましょう。

問いかけ	How long do we have to wait for a table?
正解の応答例	I'll take you to your table now.
不正解の応答例	About 10 meters.

Part 2 Question-Response

🎧 1-05〜09

最初に聞こえてくる英文に対する応答として最も適切なものを（A)〜(C）から選びましょう。

2. Mark your answer. (A) (B) (C)
3. Mark your answer. (A) (B) (C)
4. Mark your answer. (A) (B) (C)
5. Mark your answer. (A) (B) (C)

Part 3 解法のコツ 〈設問の先読み〉

設問を前もって読んでおくと、何に注意して聞けばよいのかがわかります。選択肢は飛ばしてもよいので、設問だけは先に目を通しておきましょう。

・What are the speakers discussing?

⇒「何について話しているか？」なので、会話の話題がポイント！

・What will the woman probably do next?

⇒「会話の次にどうするか？」なので、会話の後半がポイント！

Part 3 Conversations

🎧 1-10〜12

会話を聞き、6 〜 8 の設問に対する解答として最も適切なものを（A)〜(D）から選びましょう。

6. What are the speakers discussing?

(A) The cancellation of a party
(B) A banquet room at the restaurant
(C) The price of a sit-down dinner course
(D) A reservation of the whole restaurant

7. What does the woman say to the man?

(A) She is really surprised.
(B) She visited the restaurant with her husband.
(C) She enjoyed her dinner at the restaurant.
(D) She is planning to host a party.

8. Which of the following is true about the Colonel's Suite?

(A) It is not available next month.
(B) It has a seating capacity of 22 diners.
(C) It can accommodate up to 16 people standing.
(D) It is located on the top floor of the hotel.

Part 3 同様に、設問を前もって読んでおくことが重要です。設問には毎回出題される定番のものも多いですから、すぐにわかるように慣れておきましょう。また、時間に余裕があれば、設問に加え、選択肢にも目を通しておくと、その情報が理解の助けとなる場合があります。

10. What is NOT mentioned in the announcement? ⇒

(A) Seafood dishes

(B) Steaks

(C) Vegetarian dishes

(D) Pasta dishes

選択肢から料理に関する話だと推測可能！

NOT が大文字で記された設問は、「～でないものはどれか？」というタイプです！

Part 4　Talks

 1-13～15

トークを聞き、9 ～ 11 の設問に対する解答として最も適切なものを（A)～(D）から選びましょう。

9. What is Colonel Jasper's celebrating?

(A) The opening of a new restaurant

(B) Thanksgiving

(C) Its 30th anniversary

(D) The introduction of its official mascot

10. What is NOT mentioned in the announcement?

(A) Seafood dishes

(B) Steaks

(C) Vegetarian dishes

(D) Pasta dishes

11. Which of the following is true about the restaurant?

(A) Only dinner is served.

(B) It is located in downtown Brussels.

(C) It has opened in a suburban area.

(D) It is introducing a salad bar.

Communicative Training

1. Part 2 のスクリプトにある最初の問いかけを使ってパートナーと英語で互いに質問をしてみましょう。質問に答える際は、下の回答例を参考にしましょう。なお、スクリプトは教員から配布されます。

Student A
Student B（パートナー）に Part 2 のスクリプトにある最初の問いかけをしてみましょう。

Student B
Student A（パートナー）の質問に対して下の回答例を参考に答えましょう。

Q2
・彼らのウェブサイトを確認しましたか？
・まったくわかりません。
・(You choose!)

Q3
・1人（私だけ）です。
・5人です。他の人たちはすぐに来る予定です。
・(You choose!)

Q4
・いいですよ。とてもお腹がすいています。
・ごめんなさい。約束があります。
・(You choose!)

Q5
・サーロインステーキをお願いします。
・何がお勧めですか？
・(You choose!)

2. Part 3 の対話スクリプトの内容について、パートナーと英語で互いに質問をしてみましょう。質問に答える際は、対話スクリプトだけを見るようにし、下の質問は見ないようにしましょう。なお、スクリプトは教員から配布されます。

Student A
Student B（パートナー）に下記の質問をしてみましょう。

Student B
Student A（パートナー）の質問に対して Part 3 の対話スクリプトを見ながら答えましょう。

1. What is the woman planning for her husband?
2. How many people will join the party?
3. What is the date and time of the party?
4. Where will the party be held?
5. (You choose!)

Reading Section

Part 5　解法のコツ　〈品詞問題 1〉

選択肢に目を通し、（ public / publicity / publicize / publicly ）のように、ある単語の派生語が並んでいる場合は、どの品詞が入るべきかを問う「品詞問題」です。品詞問題は最もよく出てくるタイプなので、名詞、動詞、形容詞、副詞の主要 4 品詞を見分けられるようにしておくことが大切です。

✌ Check

1 〜 5 の英文中で下線を引いた単語とその品詞を線で結びましょう。ただし、複数の単語が該当する品詞があります。

1. This information is confidential and is not <u>publicly</u> available.　•　　• 名詞（Noun）
2. Eric did a series of interviews to <u>publicize</u> his new book.　•　　• 動詞（Verb）
3. The restaurant opened last week and needs a lot of <u>publicity</u>. •　　• 形容詞（Adjective）
4. This project is funded by <u>public</u> donation.　•　　• 副詞（Adverb）
5. The museum is free and open to the <u>public</u>.　•

Part 5　Incomplete Sentences

英文を完成させるのに最も適切な語句を（A）〜（D）から選びましょう。

1. I'd like to recommend Ms. Jones for the position of sous-chef as she has done a very ------- job at her current position.

   (A) satisfy
   (B) satisfaction
   (C) satisfactory
   (D) satisfactorily

2. Samuel writes restaurant reviews for various food industry ------- .

   (A) periodicals
   (B) periodic
   (C) periodically
   (D) periodical

3. We enjoyed the dinner very much but had an ------- with the server about the bill.

   (A) argue
   (B) arguable
   (C) arguably
   (D) argument

4. Mr. Kim refused to ------- about the sudden closure of the restaurant.

   (A) speculative
   (B) speculation
   (C) speculate
   (D) speculators

5. The hotel's new Chinese restaurant serves good food at ------- prices.

   (A) afford
   (B) affordability
   (C) affordably
   (D) affordable

6. This restaurant has a fine reputation and offers a wide variety of local ------- .

   (A) specialties
   (B) special
   (C) specialize
   (D) specialist

18

7. Mr. Brown ------- gives lectures on
French cuisine for those who want to
become a chef.

(A) regular
(B) regularly
(C) regularity
(D) regulation

Part 6　解法のコツ　　〈文挿入問題 1〉

形式は Part 5 と似ており、語彙・文法問題が中心ですが、空所に当てはまる文を選ぶ「文挿入問題」が 4 問中 1 問含まれます。文挿入問題は、直前や直後の文にうまくつながるかがポイントなので、直前や直後の文を注意して読みましょう。

Some of our top-ten are established and fairly well-known businesses, but half the list is made up of new entries. ------- .
　　　　　　　　　　　　　　　　　　10.

直前や直後の文がポイント！

文挿入問題

Part 6　Text Completion

次の英文を読み、空所に入れるのに最も適切な語句や文を（A）〜（D）から選びましょう。

Questions 8-11 refer to the following Web page.

Review Awards

Our reviewers have been out and about in search of the finest dining in our city. We're so fortunate to be able to enjoy a rich ------- of cuisines and
　　　　　　　　　　　　　　　　　　　　　　　　　　　　8.
influences, and we've put together the ultimate guide so that you too can enjoy some of the hidden and not-so-hidden gems. Some of our top-ten are established and fairly well-known businesses, but half the list is made up of new entries. ------- .
　　　　　　　　9.

At number ten, a new dining experience at Pisang-pisang, where chef Marco ------- Indonesian-inspired flavors to create dishes that will live in your
　　10.
memory long after your meal ends. From sides to desserts, each and every dish is an unforgettable treat, while their tasting menu is quite simply irresistible. Book early for Pisang-pisang, ------- they are often booked out a
　　　　　　　　　　　　　　　　　　　　　　　11.
month or more in advance.

At number nine, …

8. (A) select
   (B) selection
   (C) selective
   (D) selectivity

9. (A) So, you may want to search for a better place.
   (B) That's why you're chosen as the best reviewer.
   (C) However, you're encouraged to submit your own reviews.
   (D) So, with no further ado, here are our top ten.

10. (A) catches on
    (B) takes after
    (C) draws on
    (D) gets away with

11. (A) as
    (B) so
    (C) unless
    (D) until

Part 7 解法のコツ 〈語彙問題〉

長文が 1 つだけ提示され、それについて 2 ～ 4 問の設問に答える形式のシングルパッセージ問題は、全体で 10 セット出題されます。英文の内容に関する問題が中心になりますが、同義語を選ぶ語彙問題も出題されることがあります。語彙問題は次のような形式なので慣れておきましょう。

13. The word "heyday" in paragraph 3, line 2, is closest in meaning to

   (A) beginning
   (B) prime
   (C) favor
   (D) interest

「～に意味が最も近い」という意味です。

Part 7 Reading Comprehension

次の英文を読み、設問に対する答えとして最も適切なものを（A)～（D) から選びましょう。

Questions 12-15 refer to the following review.

La Taberna Miguel

2,177 reviews
Reviewed yesterday

By Isak Rossi

Don't eat here — poor service and poor cooking, a tourist-trap.

We have never eaten a paella as bad as this and at 32 euros per person, it's highly overpriced and extremely poor value for money. We ordered a starter of gambas al ajillo, and a mixed paella. They took ages to arrive, and in the end, both came at the same time. Luckily we didn't order dessert! By the time it arrived, the oil with the shrimp was already cold, and the bread was dry and stale. Our main dish, the mixed paella with chicken and seafood, felt like it had been reheated. The rice was dry, the seafood was rubbery, and there were small chicken bones in the dish. We've eaten paella many times before, but we have never eaten such a bad one. You can get better value at a supermarket food court. We complained to the server, but the manager didn't even bother to come and see us.

On top of this, they wouldn't give us a table on the terrace when it was less than one-third full. The staff are inattentive and inefficient. Everything was disappointing; they weren't even friendly or welcoming to our children.

We know this is a restaurant with a long history, and maybe in its heyday it was better. It seems very proud of its listing in the famous restaurant guidebook, but unfortunately, now, it's only a tourist trap and a rip-off. We will never set foot in it again.

12. What kind of restaurant is La Taberna Miguel?

(A) A cheap fast food restaurant
(B) A seafood food truck
(C) A renowned Spanish restaurant
(D) A buffet-style restaurant

13. What does Mr. Rossi discuss in his review?

(A) The speed of service
(B) The variety of dishes on the menu
(C) The taste of the dessert
(D) The location of the restaurant

14. The word "heyday" in paragraph 3, line 2, is closest in meaning to

(A) beginning
(B) prime
(C) favor
(D) interest

15. Which of the following is NOT true about La Taberna Miguel?

(A) It is listed in the famous restaurant guidebook.
(B) It has a long history.
(C) It has outside tables.
(D) It is proud of being a tourist trap.

Communicative Training

Part 7 で取り上げたウェブページを使ってパートナーと英語で互いに質問をしてみましょう。
答える際は、"Yes." や "No." だけで終わらないよう適宜、情報を追加しましょう。

Student A
Student B（パートナー）に下記の質問をしてみましょう。

Student B
Student A（パートナー）の質問に対して Part 7 の英文を見ながら答えましょう。

1. Who wrote this review?
2. Does he recommend the restaurant?
3. Does the restaurant have a long history?
4. How many people posted their reviews about it?
5. (You choose!)

UNIT 02 Offices

AB CD Vocabulary

1. 1 〜 10 の語句の意味として適切なものを a 〜 j の中から選びましょう。 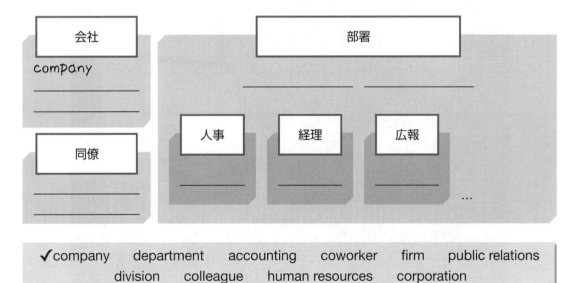 1-16

1. branch	_____	a.	契約、契約書
2. proposal	_____	b.	倉庫
3. furnished	_____	c.	現地（現場）での
4. refurbish	_____	d.	〜を誇りにする、自慢する
5. on-site	_____	e.	施設、設備
6. workshop	_____	f.	支店、営業所
7. facility	_____	g.	家具付きの
8. boast	_____	h.	改装する
9. contract	_____	i.	提案
10. warehouse	_____	j.	講習会、研修

2. 語群の中から適切な語句を選び、「会社」、「同僚」、「部署」に関する関連語の表を完成させましょう。

会社

company

_____

_____

同僚

_____

_____

部署

_____   _____

人事

_____

経理

_____

広報

_____

...

✓company   department   accounting   coworker   firm   public relations
division   colleague   human resources   corporation

23

Listening Section

Part 1 　解法のコツ　〈物の位置〉

〈人物（1人、複数）〉、〈物〉、〈風景〉という3つのパターンのうち、〈物〉が中心の写真の場合には、その「位置」と「状態」を確認しましょう。位置関係は、前置詞がポイントになります。

Check

枠の中から適切な前置詞（句）を選び、1〜4の英文を完成させましょう。

1. A cup is (　　　　　) a laptop.
2. A laptop is (　　　　　) a cup and some notebooks.
3. A pencil has been left (　　　　　) an open notebook.
4. Some notebooks are placed (　　　　　) an open notebook.

above	behind	on the corner of	
beside	between	on	under

Part 1　Photographs

1-17, 18

(A)〜(D) の英文を聞き、写真を最も適切に描写しているものを選びましょう。

1.

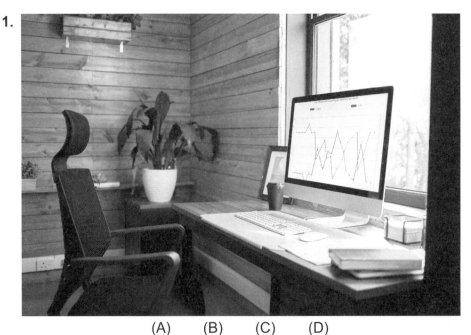

(A)　　(B)　　(C)　　(D)

Yes か No かで答えることが可能な疑問文（Yes / No 疑問文）も Wh 疑問文と並んでよく出題されます。「よくわかりません」のように、応答は必ずしも Yes / No で始まるとは限らないので注意しましょう。

問いかけ	Do you think we should hire more people?
正解の応答例	Well, I'm not sure.

Part 2　Question-Response　　🎧 1-19～23

最初に聞こえてくる英文に対する応答として最も適切なものを（A）～（C）から選びましょう。

2. Mark your answer.　　(A)　　(B)　　(C)
3. Mark your answer.　　(A)　　(B)　　(C)
4. Mark your answer.　　(A)　　(B)　　(C)
5. Mark your answer.　　(A)　　(B)　　(C)

Part 3　解法のコツ　　〈意図を問う設問〉

設問の中には、会話で使われた表現を引用し、「～と言う時、男性は何を意味していますか？」のように、話者の意図を尋ねるものがあります。文字どおりの意味ではなく、会話の文脈の中でその表現がどのように使われているかをよく考えましょう。また、こうした設問には次のようないくつかのパターンがあります。

・What does the man mean when he says "Oh, I'm sure she's on top of it"?
　　⇒「何を意味しているのか？」
・What does the man imply when he says "Oh, I'm sure she's on top of it"?
　　⇒「何をほのめかしているのか？」
・Why does the man say "Oh, I'm sure she's on top of it"?
　　⇒「なぜ～と言うのか？」

Part 3　Conversations　　🎧 1-24～26

会話を聞き、6 ～ 8 の設問に対する解答として最も適切なものを（A）～（D）から選びましょう。

6. Who most likely is Sarah?

(A) Their client
(B) Their colleague
(C) Their boss
(D) Their potential customer

7. What does the man mean when he says, "Oh, I'm sure she's on top of it"?

(A) She is on the top floor.
(B) She gets the highest salary.
(C) She will not forget her appointments.
(D) She is in control of the situation.

8. What will the man probably do next?

(A) Hand in the Bianchi contract
(B) Go over the Bianchi contract
(C) Contact Sarah
(D) Send a package to Sarah

1人の話し手によるトークには、電話のメッセージやラジオ放送、店内放送など、様々な種類が登場します。実際の問題ではトークが始まる前に次のような指示文が読まれるので、そこでトークの種類がわかります。トークの種類によって内容をある程度推測できるので、慣れておきましょう。

Questions 71-73 refer to the following telephone message.

「～に関するものだ」という意味です。

トークの種類が示されます。

✌ Check

1～5の英文中で下線を引いた語句とその日本語訳を線で結びましょう。

1. **Questions XXX-XXX** refer to the following advertisement. •   • 講習会の抜粋

2. **Questions XXX-XXX** refer to the following excerpt from a meeting. •   • 放送

3. **Questions XXX-XXX** refer to the following broadcast. •   • 会議の抜粋

4. **Questions XXX-XXX** refer to the following excerpt from a workshop. •   • お知らせ

5. **Questions XXX-XXX** refer to the following announcement. •   • 広告

Part 4 Talks

 1-27～29

トークを聞き、9～11の設問に対する解答として最も適切なものを（A）～（D）から選びましょう。

9. Who most likely are the listeners?

(A) Cleaning staff
(B) Collectors of antique furniture
(C) Hardware store owners
(D) Employees working in the warehouse

10. According to the speaker, what will happen this weekend?

(A) Some areas will be renovated.
(B) The common room will be removed.
(C) Machinery will be upgraded.
(D) The whole warehouse will be refurbished.

11. What are the listeners asked to do?

(A) Remove their lockers
(B) Take out all items from their lockers
(C) Dispose of all personal items after one week
(D) Gather at the common room at 6:00 P.M.

Communicative Training

1. Part 2 のスクリプトにある最初の問いかけを使ってパートナーと英語で互いに質問をしてみましょう。質問に答える際は、下の回答例を参考にしましょう。なお、スクリプトは教員から配布されます。

Student A

Student B（パートナー）に Part 2 のスクリプトにある最初の問いかけをしてみましょう。

Student B

Student A（パートナー）の質問に対して下の回答例を参考に答えましょう。

Q2
- いいえ、まだです。すみません。
- いいえ、すぐにします。
- (You choose!)

Q3
- もちろんです。何についてですか？
- すみません、先約があります。
- (You choose!)

Q4
- えっ？　それは昨日開かれましたよ。
- よくわかりません。すみません。
- (You choose!)

Q5
- いいえ、私が担当です。
- よくわかりません。他の人にきいてもらえませんか？
- (You choose!)

2. Part 3 の対話スクリプトの内容について、パートナーと英語で互いに質問をしてみましょう。質問に答える際は、対話スクリプトだけを見るようにし、下の質問は見ないようにしましょう。なお、スクリプトは教員から配布されます。

Student A

Student B（パートナー）に下記の質問をしてみましょう。

Student B

Student A（パートナー）の質問に対して Part 3 の対話スクリプトを見ながら答えましょう。

1. Who does the woman want to see?
2. Is Sarah Farid's colleague or client?
3. Does the woman want to ask her about the Bianchi contract?
4. According to the man, is Sarah aware of the legal situation?
5. (You choose!)

Reading Section

Part 5 解法のコツ　〈動詞の形問題1〉

選択肢に目を通し、(make / has made / is making / made) のように、ある動詞の活用形が並んでいる場合は、動詞の形を問う問題です。動詞の形を問う問題は、時制を問うものと、態（受動態かそれとも能動態か）を問うものの2種類に分けられますが、時制の場合、時を表す語句（now や last night など）が決め手になります。

👆 Check

1～4の英文中のカッコ内から正しい語句を選び○で囲みましょう。

1. Oh, there you are! The manager (has been looking / looks) for you since this morning.
2. Ms. Lewis (has returned / will be returning) from a business trip in Canada next week.
3. The Seattle branch (opens / opened) exactly one year ago today.
4. Our new office (will be / is) completed in three weeks.

Part 5 Incomplete Sentences

英文を完成させるのに最も適切な語句を（A）～（D）から選びましょう。

1. The letter ------- Mr. Lee to report to headquarters immediately.

(A) instructed
(B) instruct
(C) have instructed
(D) was instructed

2. All staff members ------- to attend the opening ceremony of the new branch.

(A) obligate
(B) are obligating
(C) are obligated
(D) have obligated

3. Recommendations from two previous employers helped ------- his credibility.

(A) established
(B) to establish
(C) establishing
(D) were established

4. We ------- trouble accessing one of our bank accounts electronically since last week.

(A) had
(B) were having
(C) have been having
(D) will have

5. The proposals that you have put forward ------- serious consideration.

(A) deserve
(B) to deserve
(C) are deserved
(D) deserving

6. Large manufacturers ------- to internationalize their operations.

(A) have been encouraging
(B) encouraged
(C) have been encouraged
(D) encourage

28

7. We'll notify you by e-mail as soon
as the new vice president ------- .

(A) arrives
(B) is going to arrive
(C) arrived
(D) will arrive

Part 6 解法のコツ 〈文書種類の把握〉

Part 6 では、手紙や e メール、メモ、広告、通知、指示など、様々な種類の文書が登場します。文書の種類によって書式上の特徴があるので、文書の種類を即座に掴むことが重要です。また、実際の問題では次のような指示文が記載されるので、そこで文書の種類がわかります。

Questions 131-134 refer to the following Web page. 　文書の種類が示されます。

✐ Check

1 ～ 5 の英文中で下線を引いた単語とその日本語訳を線で結びましょう。

1. **Questions XXX-XXX** refer to the following advertisement. ・　　・記事
2. **Questions XXX-XXX** refer to the following brochure. ・　　・通知
3. **Questions XXX-XXX** refer to the following article. ・　　・パンフレット
4. **Questions XXX-XXX** refer to the following notice. ・　　・指示
5. **Questions XXX-XXX** refer to the following instructions. ・　　・広告

Part 6 Text Completion

次の英文を読み、空所に入れるのに最も適切な語句や文を（A）～（D）から選びましょう。

Questions 8-11 refer to the following notice.

Notification of Routine Building Maintenance

Please be aware that routine building maintenance will be carried out over the weekend of July 17th/18th. This ------- restrictions of access to certain areas of the building and potentially, brief power cuts.
8.

Should you wish to receive a more detailed schedule and ------- of the work due to be undertaken, please contact the Management Office at
9.
<management@centrepoint.uk>. ------- every effort will be made to minimize
10.
inconvenience, some disruption may occur. ------- .
11.

29

8. (A) will be involved
   (B) will involve
   (C) has involved
   (D) involved

9. (A) describe
   (B) descriptive
   (C) descriptively
   (D) description

10. (A) While
    (B) Because
    (C) If
    (D) Until

11. (A) We are looking forward to the weekend of July 17th/18th.
    (B) We received your feedback with much appreciation.
    (C) We kindly request your understanding and cooperation.
    (D) Please disregard all alarms and do not evacuate the building at this time.

Part 7　解法のコツ　〈文挿入問題〉

指定の文に対して最も適した挿入箇所を選ぶ「文挿入問題」は、前後の文脈を見極めなければならず、他の問題に比べて難易度が高いです。そのため、解答するのを最後に回すのも1つの手です。また、文挿入問題は次のような形式なので、慣れておきましょう。

10. In which of the positions marked [1], [2], [3], and [4] does the following sentence best belong?

"Workspaces have excellent lighting and are soundproofed for your privacy."

(A) [1]

(B) [2]

(C) [3]

(D) [4]

> この文が入る適切な位置を [1]〜[4] から選びます。

Part 7　Reading Comprehension

次の英文を読み、設問に対する答えとして最も適切なものを（A）〜（D）から選びましょう。

Questions 12-15 refer to the following advertisement.

Hyperdesk Serviced Office Rentals in Morgan House
Office space from $1,000/month ($1,100 incl. tax)

=RENT=

Hyperdesk Office Rentals is proud to announce its latest office space, Morgan House.

Morgan House is an impressive 8-story tower block in the heart of the central business district. — [1] —. It boasts an elegant reception area and a wide choice of clean, bright office rentals. Easily accessible by car and public transport (a minute's walk from Central Station and just 20 minutes by car from the airport), it has ample parking, and is your most convenient and best-value choice for a serviced office rental.

Rental space currently available on the sixth, seventh and eighth floors of Morgan House comprises almost 1,500 square meters of private office, meeting and coworking space. Hyperdesk's Serviced Offices are fully furnished and include access to our support services.

- **Luxury surroundings**: Our offices are furnished to the highest standards. — [2] —.
- **Internet, Wi-Fi and printing**: Our on-site IT support team guarantees you fast, secure connections and reliable high-quality photocopiers for network printing. — [3] —.
- **Spacious offices**: All offices can accommodate up to 10 employees in workspaces that are far above market standards.
- **Seating options**: — [4] —. We are equipped to offer a variety of layout options. Just let us know your needs and we'll meet them.
- **Additional Facilities**: Our communal lounge areas offer gourmet coffee, beverage facilities, and a great place to network with like-minded professionals. Our basement has an on-site mini-gym with shower facilities.

12. What is indicated about Morgan House?

(A) Its rental space is supplied with furniture.
(B) It is a 5-minute walk from the Central Station.
(C) It is located on the outskirts of the city.
(D) The whole building is available to rent.

13. The word "ample" in paragraph 2, line 6, is closest in meaning to

(A) free
(B) cramped
(C) spacious
(D) expensive

14. In which of the positions marked [1], [2], [3], and [4] does the following sentence best belong?
"Workspaces have excellent lighting and are soundproofed for your privacy."

(A) [1]
(B) [2]
(C) [3]
(D) [4]

15. What is available in the communal lounge area?

(A) A sports gym
(B) Optical networking equipment
(C) On-site IT support
(D) Drinks

Communicative Training

Part 7 で取り上げた広告を使ってパートナーと英語で互いに質問をしてみましょう。答える際は、"Yes." や "No." だけで終わらないよう適宜、情報を追加しましょう。

Student A

Student B（パートナー）に下記の質問をしてみましょう。

Student B

Student A（パートナー）の質問に対して Part 7 の英文を見ながら答えましょう。

1. How many floors does Morgan House have?
2. Is it far from Central Station?
3. Does it have a parking lot?
4. What floors are available for rent?
5.（You choose!）

UNIT 03 Daily Life

Vocabulary

1. 1 ～ 10 の語句の意味として適切なものを a ～ j の中から選びましょう。　<inline_image page_ref="CD 1-30" />

1. compliment	＿＿＿	a．大げさに言う、誇張する
2. merchandise	＿＿＿	b．気前の良い
3. incident	＿＿＿	c．信頼できる
4. reliable	＿＿＿	d．（製品の）保証（書）
5. insurance	＿＿＿	e．重要な
6. generous	＿＿＿	f．事件、出来事
7. significant	＿＿＿	g．探偵、刑事
8. warranty	＿＿＿	h．商品、品物
9. detective	＿＿＿	i．保険
10. exaggerate	＿＿＿	j．～を称賛する

2. 語群の中から適切な日本語訳を選び、派生語の図を完成させましょう。

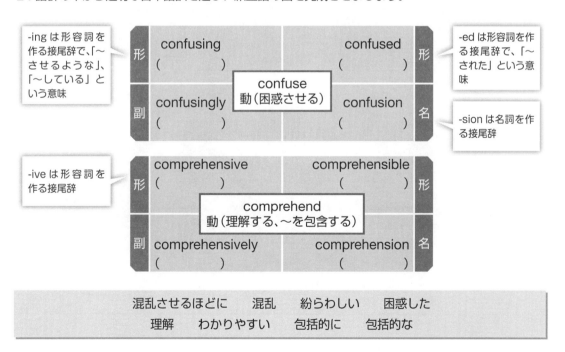

-ing は形容詞を作る接尾辞で、「～させるような」、「～している」という意味

形　confusing （　　　）

形　confused （　　　）　-ed は形容詞を作る接尾辞で、「～された」という意味

confuse 動（困惑させる）

副　confusingly （　　　）

名　confusion （　　　）　-sion は名詞を作る接尾辞

-ive は形容詞を作る接尾辞

形　comprehensive （　　　）

形　comprehensible （　　　）

comprehend 動（理解する、～を包含する）

副　comprehensively （　　　）

名　comprehension （　　　）

混乱させるほどに　　混乱　　紛らわしい　　困惑した
理解　　わかりやすい　　包括的に　　包括的な

| Part 1 | 解法のコツ | 〈人物（2人）の描写〉 |

2人の人物が写っている写真の場合、「向かい合っている」や「並んでいる」のように、位置関係を
確認しましょう。

They're facing each other.
（彼らは向かい合っています）

They're walking side by side.
（彼らは並んで歩いています）

They're looking in the
same direction.
（彼らは同じ方向を見ています）

| Part 1 | Photographs |

🎧 1-31, 32

(A)〜(D) の英文を聞き、写真を最も適切に描写しているものを選びましょう。

1.

(A)　　(B)　　(C)　　(D)

最初の問いかけに出てきた単語が入った選択肢は不正解である場合がほとんどです。問いかけが理解できなかった受験者は、選択肢の中に問いかけに使われていた単語が聞こえるとついその選択肢を選ぶ傾向があるため、出題者は意図的に不正解の選択肢として用意しているのです。

問いかけ	Tell me what's on your mind.
不正解の応答例	Don't worry. I don't mind.
正解の応答例	Well, I'm thinking of quitting my job.

Part 2 Question-Response

🎧 1-33〜37

最初に聞こえてくる英文に対する応答として最も適切なものを（A）〜（C）から選びましょう。

2. Mark your answer.　(A)　(B)　(C)
3. Mark your answer.　(A)　(B)　(C)
4. Mark your answer.　(A)　(B)　(C)
5. Mark your answer.　(A)　(B)　(C)

Part 3 解法のコツ 〈理由を問う設問〉

理由を尋ねる設問では、"Why did the man arrive late?" のように why で始まるものが定番です。会話の中の発言を取り上げ、その発言をした理由を問うタイプもあるので慣れておきましょう。また、選択肢は "He missed his train." のような文タイプか、"To surprise the woman" のような不定詞のタイプとなります。不定詞タイプの選択肢は短いものが多いので、できるだけ会話を聞く前に選択肢まで見ておくようにしましょう。会話のヒントが得られます。

8. Why does the man say, "You can say that again"?
　　(A) To compliment the woman
　　(B) To accept an apology
　　(C) To agree with the woman
　　(D) To express surprise

会話の中に出てくる発言です。

不定詞タイプの選択肢は短いものが多いです。

Part 3 Conversations

🎧 1-38〜40

会話を聞き、6 〜 8 の設問に対する解答として最も適切なものを（A）〜（D）から選びましょう。

6. What is the problem?

(A) A missing warranty
(B) Expiration of the warranty period
(C) Damaged flooring
(D) A leaking kitchen faucet

7. What does the man say they will have to do?

(A) Use their own insurance
(B) Pay for the repairs
(C) Buy a new fridge
(D) Return the call from Holton's

8. Why does the man say, "You can say that again"?

(A) To compliment the woman
(B) To accept an apology
(C) To agree with the woman
(D) To express surprise

留守番電話のメッセージには、下記のような基本的な流れがあるので、情報がどのような順序で出てくるか予測することができます。慣れておきましょう。

1. 自己紹介	Hi, Scott. This is Jennifer.	
	⇒氏名の連絡（会社名が入る場合もある）	
2. 目的	I just wanted to let you know that the delivery from the office supply store arrived this morning.	
	⇒商品配達のお知らせ	
3. 追加情報、注意事項	I checked the package and found that the web camera was missing.	
	⇒欠品があったことの連絡	
4. 依頼事項* *必要な場合のみ	Just call me back and let me know. My number is 555-2150. Thank you.	
	⇒連絡先の通知	

Part 4　Talks　　1-41～43

トークを聞き、9 ～ 11 の設問に対する解答として最も適切なものを（A)～（D）から選びましょう。

9. Who most likely is Julie?

(A) The speaker's mother
(B) The speaker's sister
(C) A careworker
(D) A driver

10. According to the speaker, what is the problem?

(A) No one is available to support their mother.
(B) The healthcare support service went out of business.
(C) Their mother's meal has not been delivered yet.
(D) Their mother had an accident.

11. What is the listener asked to do?

(A) Call the healthcare support service
(B) Call in on the speaker
(C) Get dressed soon
(D) Return the call

Communicative Training

1. Part 2 のスクリプトにある最初の問いかけを使ってパートナーと英語で互いに質問をして
   みましょう。質問に答える際は、下の回答例を参考にしましょう。なお、スクリプトは教
   員から配布されます。

Student A
Student B（パート
ナー）に Part 2 の
スクリプトにある最
初の問いかけをして
みましょう。

Student B
Student A（パート
ナー）の質問に対し
て下の回答例を参考
に答えましょう。

Q2
・彼は大学生です。
・彼は探偵です。
・(You choose!)

Q3
・ありがとう。助かります。
・ありがとう。でも、（それらは）そんなに重
　くないから1人で運べます。
・(You choose!)

Q4
・はい、彼が私に話してくれました。
・もちろんです。彼がその仕事を見つけるのを
　助けてあげましたから。
・(You choose!)

Q5
・はい、学芸員*をしています。　*curator
・いいえ。どうしてそんなことを聞くのですか？
・(You choose!)

2. Part 3 の対話スクリプトの内容について、パートナーと英語で互いに質問をしてみましょ
   う。質問に答える際は、対話スクリプトだけを見るようにし、下の質問は見ないようにし
   ましょう。なお、スクリプトは教員から配布されます。

Student A
Student B（パート
ナー）に下記の質問
をしてみましょう。

Student B
Student A（パート
ナー）の質問に対し
て Part 3 の対話ス
クリプトを見ながら
答えましょう。

1. Who did the man get a call from?
2. What did he learn about the fridge?
3. Do the man and woman have to pay for the parts and repairs?
4. What does the man mean when he says, "You can say that again"?
5. (You choose!)

Reading Section

Part 5　解法のコツ　〈品詞問題2〉

品詞問題で問われる品詞は、主に名詞、動詞、形容詞、副詞の4つです。形容詞と副詞は共に「説明を加える」役割を果たすため区別が難しいですが、確実に見分けられるようにしましょう。形容詞と副詞を見分けるポイントは次のとおりです。

形容詞	名詞に説明を加えます。 ex.) We had a **wonderful** dinner . / The dinner was **great**.
副　詞	名詞以外（動詞、形容詞、副詞など）に説明を加えます。 ex.) I **completely** forgot that the report was due today.

✌ Check

網掛けの語に注意して1〜4の英文中のカッコ内から正しい語を選び○で囲みましょう。

1. Joseph was (repeated / repeatedly) warned not to work too hard.

2. Mr. & Mrs. Smith made a (generous / generously) donation to charity.

3. We were (confused / confusedly) when the project manager left the company all of a sudden.

4. Fill out this form (complete / completely) and send it back to me as soon as possible.

Part 5　Incomplete Sentences

英文を完成させるのに最も適切な語句を（A）〜（D）から選びましょう。

1. Professor Mason claimed his remarks about the incident had been reported ------- .

(A) more inaccurate
(B) inaccurately
(C) inaccuracy
(D) inaccurate

2. I don't believe what Bruce says because he always exaggerates to make his stories more ------- .

(A) amusing
(B) amusingly
(C) amuse
(D) amusement

3. When it comes to choosing photographic equipment, portability is as important as ------- .

(A) reliably
(B) rely
(C) reliability
(D) reliable

4. It is often said that a good diet ------- lessens the risk of heart disease.

(A) significant
(B) significantly
(C) signify
(D) significance

38

5. At the meeting they presented a detailed and ------- analysis of children's emotions.

(A) careful
(B) care
(C) cared
(D) carefully

6. At the store, the merchandise is ------- displayed and the sales clerks are friendly and helpful.

(A) attractive
(B) attract
(C) attractiveness
(D) attractively

7. Another solution, which I strongly ------- , is to lower taxes for everyone.

(A) favorable
(B) favor
(C) favorably
(D) to favor

Part 6 解法のコツ 〈解答の順序〉

文挿入問題は語句挿入問題と比べると難易度が高いため、時間との勝負になる実際の試験では、解答の順序を最後にしたほうが得策です。文章の途中に文挿入問題があると、つい空所の順番に解きたくなりますが、語句挿入問題を優先したほうが良いでしょう。リーディングセクションでは、Part 5 ～ 6 にあまり時間をかけず、大量の英文を読まなければならない Part 7 にできるだけ多くの時間をかけるのが鉄則です。

The ------- actor's wife, Jennifer Carter, posted on Flitter, "Our hearts are broken.
8.
------- . He was the love of my life, and one of the greatest performers on the screen
9.
and stage."

実際の試験では、9 の文挿入問題より 10 の語句挿入問題を先に解きましょう。

Carter was born in Brooklyn, New York, and appeared in a ------- of roles.
10.

Part 6 Text Completion

次の英文を読み、空所に入れるのに最も適切な語句や文を（A）～（D）から選びましょう。

Questions 8-11 refer to the following article.

(May 8) Dave Carter, award-winning star of films like *Murder on the Island* and the Broadway musical *Last Dance*, died Tuesday of lung cancer, at his home in Naples, Florida. He was 73.

The ------- actor's wife, Jennifer Carter, posted on Flitter, "Our hearts are
8.
broken. ------- . He was the love of my life, and one of the greatest performers
9.
on the screen and stage."

Carter was born in Brooklyn, New York, and appeared in a ------- of roles. Carter
10.
earned a Tony nomination for his role in *Last Dance* and appeared in a long
list of movies that ------- *Death on the Seine* and *The XYZ Murders*. His best-
11.
known role is detective Pete Fletcher in Chuck Wilder's *Murder on the Island*.

8. (A) iconic
   (B) anonymous
   (C) obscure
   (D) fledgling

9. (A) We're thrilled to pieces at the news.
   (B) Our father died peacefully in his sleep at home today.
   (C) There will never be another Dave Carter.
   (D) It would certainly be a great honor.

10. (A) variation
    (B) various
    (C) vary
    (D) variety

11. (A) including
    (B) included
    (C) was included
    (D) will include

Part 7　解法のコツ　〈チャット書式1〉

Part 6 ～ 7 では手紙やメモ、広告、通知など、様々な種類の文書が登場しますが、Part 7 特有な形式としてオンラインチャットが挙げられます。次のような指示文が記載され、1 ～ 2 問出題されます。

Questions 147-148 refer to the following text-message chain.
Questions 161-164 refer to the following online discussion.

また、チャット特有の問題として、「〇時〇分に、●●さんは～と書いていますが、どういう意味でしょうか？」のように、チャットで使われた表現を引用し、話者の意図を尋ねるものがあります。

- At 2:45 P.M., what does Marc most likely mean when he writes, "Oh well, there are others"?

引用された表現の文字どおりの意味ではなく、チャットのやりとりの中でどのように使われているかをよく考えて答えるようにしましょう。

Part 7　Reading Comprehension

次の英文を読み、設問に対する答えとして最も適切なものを（A）～（D）から選びましょう。

Questions 12-15 refer to the following text-message chain.

MARC [2:30 P.M.]
Hey there, any clearer about your visit plans?

OLIVER [2:33 P.M.]
Thanks for your offer of staying over. I have a reservation at the Palace Hotel for Friday through Sunday, but I can cancel my reservation free of charge until the 20th. Can I let you know by tomorrow? Kayla is in town, so I want to see her. And Paul is up for Saturday night dinner, too.

MARC [2:37 P.M.]
OK, let me know your plans when you know them. If you stay at the Palace and we meet the guys in the city center, I may even be tempted to stay overnight in the city myself.

OLIVER [2:40 P.M.]
Where were you thinking of meeting for dinner with the guys on Saturday?

MARC [2:42 P.M.]
Haven't thought about evening details yet. Any preference yourself? I was thinking pizza or Spanish.

OLIVER [2:43 P.M.]
Spanish sounds good.

MARC [2:45 P.M.]
I was going to suggest this place (https://www.latabernamiguel.html), which is really good for that kind of group, but I checked the Web site and it's just closed. Oh well, there are others.

12. What is the chat discussion mainly about?

(A) Oliver's travel plan
(B) The closure of a restaurant
(C) Marc's accommodation
(D) A hotel reservation

13. According to the chat, what is indicated about the dinner on Saturday?

(A) It'll be on Marc.
(B) It's scheduled at the Palace Hotel.
(C) Oliver will make a reservation.
(D) The place for it hasn't been decided.

14. The word "tempted" in paragraph 3, line 3, is closest in meaning to

(A) imposed
(B) inclined
(C) discouraged
(D) prevented

15. At 2:45 P.M., what does Marc most likely mean when he writes, "Oh well, there are others"?

(A) He can meet them at another time.
(B) He needs to check with others.
(C) He'll be able to find another good restaurant.
(D) Others must have different ideas.

Communicative Training

Part 7 で取り上げたチャットを使ってパートナーと英語で互いに質問をしてみましょう。答える際は、"Yes." や "No." だけで終わらないよう適宜、情報を追加しましょう。

Student A
Student B（パートナー）に下記の質問をしてみましょう。

Student B
Student A（パートナー）の質問に対して Part 7 の英文を見ながら答えましょう。

1. Who has a reservation at the Palace Hotel?
2. Until when can he cancel his reservation for free?
3. What day of the week are they meeting for dinner?
4. What kind of food are they going to have?
5.（You choose!）

Personnel

📖 Vocabulary

1. 1 〜 10 の語句の意味として適切なものを a 〜 j の中から選びましょう。　💿 1-44

1. dismiss	_____		a . 信用照会先、身元照会先
2. evaluation	_____		b . 〜を解雇する
3. qualification	_____		c . 仕事量、作業量
4. reference	_____		d . 候補者
5. promotion	_____		e . 評価、査定
6. workload	_____		f . 辞任する
7. resign	_____		g . 昇進
8. properly	_____		h . 履歴書
9. candidate	_____		i . 資格、必要条件
10. résumé	_____		j . 適切に、ちゃんと

2. 語群の中から適切な日本語訳を選び、派生語の図を完成させましょう。

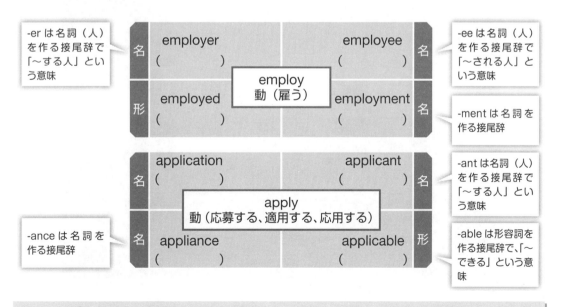

-er は名詞（人）を作る接尾辞で「〜する人」という意味

名　employer
（　　　　　）

名　employee
（　　　　　）

-ee は名詞（人）を作る接尾辞で「〜される人」という意味

employ
動（雇う）

形　employed
（　　　　　）

名　employment
（　　　　　）

-ment は名詞を作る接尾辞

名　application
（　　　　　）

名　applicant
（　　　　　）

-ant は名詞（人）を作る接尾辞で「〜する人」という意味

apply
動（応募する、適用する、応用する）

名　appliance
（　　　　　）

形　applicable
（　　　　　）

-ance は名詞を作る接尾辞

-able は形容詞を作る接尾辞で、「〜できる」という意味

雇用　　雇用された　　従業員　　雇用主　　適用できる　　応募者

電気器具　　申し込み・適用

Listening Section

| Part 1 | 解法のコツ | 〈人物（3人以上）の描写1〉 |

3人以上の人物が写っている写真の場合、「彼らは全員〜している」のように、共通点を描写するものと、「1人の男性が〜している」のように、人物の中で目立つ人物について描写するタイプとに分かれます。They'reで始まる文が聞こえた場合は、全員の共通点を描写しているかどうか確認しましょう。ただし、写真から全員の職業などが明らかな場合は、workersやtravelersのような具体的な単語が主語として使われることもあります。

Check

1〜6の語句とその日本語訳とを線で結びましょう。

1. attendee   ·   · 建設作業員
2. vendor   ·   · 歩行者
3. courier   ·   · 配管工
4. construction worker ·   · 出席者
5. pedestrian   ·   · 配達員
6. plumber   ·   · 行商人

| Part 1 | Photographs |
 1-45, 46

(A)〜(D) の英文を聞き、写真を最も適切に描写しているものを選びましょう。

1.

(A)   (B)   (C)   (D)

Yes / No 疑問文の中には、"Don't you like it?" のように文頭が否定語で始まる否定疑問文があります。日本語だと「はい、好きではありません」と答えられますが、英語の場合は、通常の疑問文であろうと否定疑問文であろうと、肯定するなら Yes、否定するなら No と答えると覚えておきましょう。

問いかけ	Haven't you applied for the position yet?
不正解の応答例	Yes, I need more time. / No, I have.
正解の応答例	No, I was too busy.

Part 2 **Question-Response** 1-47～51

最初に聞こえてくる英文に対する応答として最も適切なものを（A）～（C）から選びましょう。

2. Mark your answer.   (A)   (B)   (C)
3. Mark your answer.   (A)   (B)   (C)
4. Mark your answer.   (A)   (B)   (C)
5. Mark your answer.   (A)   (B)   (C)

時を尋ねる設問では、"When does the woman want to see the man?" のように when で始まるものが定番ですが、この他にも how often や how soon など様々な疑問詞を使って尋ねられることがありますので慣れておきましょう。

・How often does the train run?	⇒「どのくらいの間隔」で頻度がポイント！
・How long have they been waiting?	⇒「どのくらい」で時間の長さがポイント！
・How soon does the concert begin?	⇒「どのくらいすぐ」で開始時期がポイント！
・How long ago did the woman order?	⇒「どのくらい前」で過去の時期がポイント！

Part 3 **Conversations** 1-52～54

会話を聞き、6 ～ 8 の設問に対する解答として最も適切なものを（A）～（D）から選びましょう。

6. According to the woman, what is the problem?

(A) She has trouble getting along with people at work.
(B) She has to take care of her sick children.
(C) Her workload is too heavy.
(D) She hasn't got a promotion she deserves.

7. What does the woman say she is doing recently?

(A) Eating properly
(B) Sleeping properly
(C) Coping with stress
(D) Taking medicine

8. When did the woman start feeling like this?

(A) About two weeks ago
(B) About a month ago
(C) Two months ago
(D) Four months ago

商品やサービスの広告に関するトークの場合、相手の注意を引くために最初の呼びかけで概要がわかるようになっています。下記が基本的な流れなので、特に出だしに注意して聞くようにしましょう。

1. 呼びかけ	Are you looking to buy or rent a home in Ferguson, Ohio? Look no further.	
	⇒対象は家の購入や賃貸を検討している人	
2. 自己紹介	Green House is ready to help you find your dream house.	
	⇒会社の紹介	
3. 詳細	From an affordable two-bedroomed house to a luxury four-bedroomed house, we have what you need. Green House invites you to celebrate with us the opening of our newest branch in the River Oaks Mall.	
	⇒新支店開設の案内	
4. 結び	Come join us at the opening event on Sunday, June 3.	
	⇒聞き手への提案	

Part 4　Talks

1-55～57

トークを聞き、9 ～ 11 の設問に対する解答として最も適切なものを（A)～（D) から選びましょう。

9. Who is this talk directed to?

(A) People who lost their job
(B) People who wish to start their own company
(C) People who want to change jobs
(D) People who got employed recently

10. What does the speaker imply when he says, "It's never too late"?

(A) The listeners hardly have a chance.
(B) The listeners may still have a chance.
(C) The listener's case will always be dismissed.
(D) The listeners may be fired at any time.

11. What does the speaker imply when he says, "We fight for our client's rights like no other"?

(A) They often argue with their clients.
(B) They can be trusted to do a good job.
(C) They offer a reasonable price.
(D) Their clients are different from their competitors.

Communicative Training

1. Part 2 のスクリプトにある最初の問いかけを使ってパートナーと英語で互いに質問をしてみましょう。質問に答える際は、下の回答例を参考にしましょう。なお、スクリプトは教員から配布されます。

Student A
Student B（パートナー）に Part 2 のスクリプトにある最初の問いかけをしてみましょう。

Student B
Student A（パートナー）の質問に対して下の回答例を参考に答えましょう。

Q2
・はい、彼らはもうじきここに来るはずです。
・聞いていませんか？　面接は中止になりましたよ。
・(You choose!)

Q3
・はい、とても興味があります。
・実はもう応募しました。
・(You choose!)

Q4
・ええ、その通りです。
・おっしゃりたいことは分かりますが、十分な時間がありません。
・(You choose!)

Q5
・ええ、しませんでした。私にはもっと時間が必要です。
・いや、しましたよ。
・(You choose!)

2. Part 3 の対話スクリプトの内容について、パートナーと英語で互いに質問をしてみましょう。質問に答える際は、スクリプトだけを見るようにし、下の質問は見ないようにしましょう。なお、スクリプトは教員から配布されます。

Student A
Student B（パートナー）に下記の質問をしてみましょう。

Student B
Student A（パートナー）の質問に対して Part 3 の対話スクリプトを見ながら答えましょう。

1. Who has been having some trouble recently, the man or the woman?
2. Is the woman thinking about quitting her job?
3. What does she mention as the reason?
4. Is she sleeping properly?
5. (You choose!)

Reading Section

Part 5 　解法のコツ　　〈品詞問題 **3**〉

命令文などを除き、通常、英文には主語と（述語）動詞があります。品詞問題のうち名詞と動詞は、主語と（述語）動詞、そして目的語（動作の対象）という英文の基本要素を把握することが見分けるポイントです。

名　詞	人や物事などの名称を表し、主語や目的語となります。 ex.) **Applications** must be submitted by May 31. 　　 You must submit your **application** by May 31.
動　詞	主語の動作や状態を示します。 ex.) Jane **applied** for a job with the local newspaper.

☝ Check

1 ～ 4 の英文中のカッコ内から正しい語を選び○で囲みましょう。

1. (Attend / Attendance) at these lectures is not compulsory.

2. The president is under intense pressure to (resign / resignation).

3. We'd like our (employees / employ) to behave in a professional manner.

4. Keep up the struggle till you (success / succeed).

Part 5 　**Incomplete Sentences**

英文を完成させるのに最も適切な語句を（A）～（D）から選びましょう。

1. Ms. Clark's extensive résumé suggests that she is a competent ------- in her field.

   (A) specialist
   (B) special
   (C) specialized
   (D) specialize

2. Over the next few days, you are scheduled to ------- several training sessions.

   (A) attendance
   (B) attendant
   (C) attending
   (D) attend

3. The applicant showed ------- tact during the job interview.

   (A) admire
   (B) admiration
   (C) admirable
   (D) admirably

4. We are sorry to inform you that we currently have no job ------- .

   (A) vacate
   (B) vacates
   (C) vacantly
   (D) vacancies

5. Please accept this letter as ------- notice that I am resigning from the position of travel agent.

   (A) formal
   (B) formalize
   (C) formality
   (D) formally

6. I'm interested in applying for the position of network administrator that you ------- in the Sunday edition of *The Daily Telegraph*.

(A) advertisement
(B) advertiser
(C) advertised
(D) advertising

7. I would appreciate the opportunity to meet with you to discuss my ------- for your position.

(A) qualify
(B) qualified
(C) qualifier
(D) qualifications

Part 6 解法のコツ 〈定型表現 1〉

求人案内などを扱った英文では、「仕事内容には〜が含まれます」や「応募者には〜が必要です」のような定型表現が数多く登場します。こうした定型表現が語句挿入問題や文挿入問題に使われることもあるので、ぜひ慣れておきましょう。

✓ Check

1〜5の英文中で下線を引いた語句とその日本語訳を線で結びましょう。

1. Fluency in Spanish <u>is preferred but not required</u>. •   • 応募者には〜が必要です
2. <u>Applicants must have</u> a degree in tourism. •   • 職務には〜が含まれます
3. <u>Duties include</u> supervising tour guides. •   • 採用者には〜が必要です
4. <u>The successful candidate will have</u> a degree in economics. •   • 〜を募集しています
5. Ace Tours <u>has an opening for</u> enthusiastic tour guides! •   • 望ましいが必須ではありません

Part 6 Text Completion

次の英文を読み、空所に入れるのに最も適切な語句や文を（A）〜（D）から選びましょう。

Questions 8-11 refer to the following announcement.

Office Assistant Needed

A law firm in central Perth seeks an administrative assistant with at least three years of experience working in a law office. The assistant ------- to carry out a range of tasks, from simple clerical duties to complex assignments requiring some project management skills.

8.

The successful candidate must be proficient in the use of general office software. ------- , excellent verbal and written communication skills are necessary. A university degree is preferred, but candidates with secondary school certificate are also ------- .

9.

10.

Interested individuals are encouraged to send an e-mail with their résumé and the names of two references to Adam Thompson, Manager of Human Resources, at <athompson@hglegal.com>. ------- .

11.

8. (A) will be expected
   (B) expects
   (C) was expected
   (D) is expecting

9. (A) Therefore
   (B) However
   (C) In addition
   (D) For instance

10. (A) irrelevant
    (B) eligible
    (C) adjacent
    (D) consistent

11. (A) Applications received after this deadline will not be read.
    (B) If you have any questions or concerns, please feel free to contact me.
    (C) Thank you for your consideration of this request.
    (D) Applications must be submitted by July 30 at the latest.

Part 7 解法のコツ 〈eメール書式〉

Part 7 で出題される文書の中でも e メールは頻出書式の 1 つです。次の書式例で書式の特徴に慣れておきましょう。

eメールの書式例

From: To: Date: Subject: Attachment:	■ヘッダー 送信者、受信者、日付、件名、添付物が記されます。件名（Subject）は概要理解のヒントになるので必ず確認しましょう。
Dear Mr. Smith, Sincerely,	■本文 最初に、宛先（＝受信者）が記されます。Dear Mr. Smith のように、Dear から始まることが多いですが、親しい間柄の場合、Hi, Rick のようになることもあります。 次に、用件が述べられ、ここが問題の中心になるので、じっくり読みましょう。結びは、(Yours) Sincerely のほか、(Best) Regards などもよく使われます。
Ian Freely Manager Human Resources ABC Bank	■フッター 送信者の氏名、所属（役職、部署、会社名）が記されます。

次の英文を読み、設問に対する答えとして最も適切なものを（A）〜（D）から選びましょう。

Questions 12-15 refer to the following e-mail.

To:	All departments
From:	mlevin@abcbank.com (Human Resources)
Date:	June 2
Subject:	Anger Management Workshop

Dear colleagues,

As part of our ongoing efforts to create a harmonious and enjoyable working environment, all employees will be expected to take part in an anger management workshop. Participation in the workshop is mandatory and four sessions will be held over the coming months to enable everyone to attend at a convenient time. — [1] —.

Anger is a common emotion, and if not managed well, can be extremely damaging at a personal and professional level, injurious to interpersonal relationships and one's own health. — [2] —.

The workshop, which will be led by the University of Dusseldorf's Prof. Francis Furter, examines why people become angry, the dangers associated with not managing your anger, and how to work with this emotion. Employees will learn practical techniques to help them manage their anger at work, at home, and in public. — [3] —.

The dates and further details related to the workshop can be found in the "Workshop guidelines" document (attached). Click on this link to access the "Workshop attendance form" to reserve your place. — [4] —.

Sincerely,

Mark Levin
Manager
Human Resources

12. What is the purpose of the e-mail?

(A) To gather ideas for future workshops

(B) To collect data on anger management

(C) To announce a training session

(D) To encourage feedback on a workshop

13. What is indicated about the workshop?

(A) All employees have to attend it.

(B) It will be held online.

(C) The dates have yet to be decided.

(D) It will be held at the University of Dusseldorf.

14. What is the receiver of the e-mail asked to do?

(A) Register for the workshop
(B) Reserve judgment on anger
(C) Submit his or her ideas on anger management
(D) Reply to Mr. Levin

15. In which of the positions marked [1], [2], [3], and [4] does the following sentence best belong?
"But anger management is an easily learnable skill that can have benefits far beyond the workplace."

(A) [1]
(B) [2]
(C) [3]
(D) [4]

Communicative Training

Part 7 で取り上げた eメールを使ってパートナーと英語で互いに質問をしてみましょう。答える際は、"Yes." や "No." だけで終わらないよう適宜、情報を追加しましょう。

Student A
Student B（パートナー）に下記の質問をしてみましょう。

Student B
Student A（パートナー）の質問に対して Part 7 の英文を見ながら答えましょう。

1. When was this e-mail sent?
2. Who wrote it?
3. What is the workshop about?
4. Who will lead the workshop?
5. (You choose!)

UNIT 05 Shopping

 ## Vocabulary

1. 1 ～ 10 の語句の意味として適切なものを a ～ j の中から選びましょう。　　🎵 1-58

1. voucher	＿＿＿	a．〜を禁じる
2. purchase	＿＿＿	b．購入（品）、購入する
3. refund	＿＿＿	c．無料の
4. checkout	＿＿＿	d．送り状、明細付き請求書
5. inquiry	＿＿＿	e．返金
6. forbid	＿＿＿	f．（店の）レジ、精算所
7. invoice	＿＿＿	g．問い合わせ
8. issue	＿＿＿	h．（商品・サービスの）引換券
9. consecutive	＿＿＿	i．（印刷物など）を発行する
10. complimentary	＿＿＿	j．連続した

2. 語群の中から適切な日本語訳を選び、派生語の図を完成させましょう。

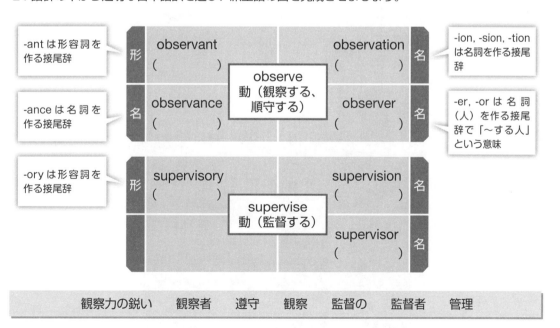

観察力の鋭い　　観察者　　遵守　　観察　　監督の　　監督者　　管理

Listening Section

人物写真の場合、その人の「動作」と「状態」を描写するのに現在進行形が多く使われます。〈am / is / are + 動詞の ing 形〉の部分を聞き逃さないようにしましょう。

👆 **Check**

下の写真の描写として最も適切な英文を 1 ～ 4 の中から選びましょう。

1. The man is taking out his credit card from his wallet.
2. The man is receiving his change from the cashier.
3. The man is passing his credit card to the cashier.
4. The man is reaching into his wallet for a credit card.

Part 1　Photographs

🎧 1-59, 60

(A) ～ (D) の英文を聞き、写真を最も適切に描写しているものを選びましょう。

1.

(A)　　(B)　　(C)　　(D)

"A or B?" という形式の選択疑問文は Yes / No では答えられないので、Yes / No で始まる選択肢は不正解となります。基本的には A か B のどちらかを選ぶ応答が正解になりますが、「どちらでもありません」や「どちらでも良いです」のような応答が正解になることもあります。

問いかけ	Would you like tea or coffee?
正解の応答例	Neither, thanks.
問いかけ	Which is better, the brown suit or the black one?
正解の応答例	Either one looks great on you.

Part 2 Question-Response

🔊 1-61〜65

最初に聞こえてくる英文に対する応答として最も適切なものを（A）〜（C）から選びましょう。

2. Mark your answer. (A) (B) (C)
3. Mark your answer. (A) (B) (C)
4. Mark your answer. (A) (B) (C)
5. Mark your answer. (A) (B) (C)

Part 3 解法のコツ 〈次の行動を問う設問〉

"What will the man probably do next?" のように、会話の後に話し手がどのような行動をするかを問う設問は頻出問題の１つです。３つある設問のうち最後の設問として登場することが多く、会話における最後の発言がポイントになるので、注意して聞き取りましょう。

・What will the man probably do next?
・What does the man ask the woman to do?
・What does the man say he will do?
・What is the man asked to do?

> 会話の最後で何と言っているかに注意しましょう！

Part 3 Conversations

🔊 1-66〜68

会話を聞き、６〜８の設問に対する解答として最も適切なものを（A）〜（D）から選びましょう。

6. What does the woman imply when she says, "You're not serious, are you"?

(A) It doesn't suit the man at all.
(B) The man doesn't wear suits very often.
(C) It is not on sale.
(D) It is too expensive.

7. What does the man say about the jacket?

(A) He likes the color.
(B) It is on sale.
(C) He prefers another jacket of a different color.
(D) The quality is excellent.

8. What will the woman probably do next?

(A) Go to the cashier
(B) Go to the fitting room
(C) Select some clothes for the man
(D) Buy a different jacket for herself

店内アナウンスには、下記のような基本的な流れがあるので、情報がどのような順序で出てくるか予測することができます。慣れておきましょう。

1. 呼びかけ	Attention, all customers.	
2. 目的	Value Mart announces today's special offers.	
	⇒特別セールのお知らせ	
3. 追加情報、注意事項	But remember these great offers are for today only and once they're gone, they're gone.	
	⇒特別セールは本日限り！	
4. 結び	Thank you for shopping with us today.	
	⇒謝辞	

Part 4 Talks

1-69〜71

トークを聞き、9 〜 11 の設問に対する解答として最も適切なものを（A)〜(D）から選びましょう。

9. What is Abode?

(A) A T-shirt brand
(B) A charity group
(C) A group of homeless people
(D) A new product

10. According to the speaker, what will the volunteers do?

(A) Sell red T-shirts
(B) Prevent theft
(C) Run a cash register
(D) Pack customers' bags

11. What does the speaker ask listeners to do?

(A) Donate some money
(B) Join Abode
(C) Bag their groceries by themselves
(D) Stand in line at the checkouts

Communicative Training

1. Part 2 のスクリプトにある最初の問いかけを使ってパートナーと英語で互いに質問をして
   みましょう。質問に答える際は、下の回答例を参考にしましょう。なお、スクリプトは教
   員から配布されます。

Student A
Student B（パート
ナー）に Part 2 の
スクリプトにある最
初の問いかけをして
みましょう。

Student B
Student A（パート
ナー）の質問に対し
て下の回答例を参考
に答えましょう。

Q2
・私が彼に返金を求めました。
・あなたがそうしてもらえませんか？
・(You choose!)

Q3
・あなたたちと一緒に行きたいです。
・私は家にいたいです。
・(You choose!)

Q4
・現金で支払います。
・クレジットカードで支払います。
・(You choose!)

Q5
・私は茶色の方が好きですね。
・どちらもあなたによく似合いますよ。
・(You choose!)

---

2. Part 3 の対話スクリプトの内容について、パートナーと英語で互いに質問をしてみましょ
   う。質問に答える際は、対話スクリプトだけを見るようにし、下の質問は見ないようにし
   ましょう。なお、スクリプトは教員から配布されます。

Student A
Student B（パート
ナー）に下記の質問
をしてみましょう。

Student B
Student A（パート
ナー）の質問に対し
て Part 3 の対話ス
クリプトを見ながら
答えましょう。

1. According to the man, is the jacket on sale?
2. Does the woman think that it suits him?
3. Who says, "You're kidding!"?
4. What does the woman say she'll do for him?
5. (You choose!)

| Part 5 | 解法のコツ | 〈動詞の形問題 2〉 |

動詞の形を問う問題は時制を問うものが中心ですが、態（受動態かそれとも能動態か）を問うものも含まれます。受動態かそれとも能動態かを問うだけであれば 2 択ですが、実際の問題では選択肢が 4 つありますので、惑わされないようにしましょう。

能動態	「～は…する」のように、何かに働きかける意味を表します。 ex.) I'm attaching the picture of the cracked plate to this e-mail.
受動態	「～は…される／されている」のように、何らかの動作を受ける意味を表します。 ex.) The picture of the cracked plate is attached to this e-mail.

Check

1 ～ 4 の英文中のカッコ内から正しい語句を選び○で囲みましょう。

1. Tickets must (purchase / be purchased) at least two weeks in advance.
2. Pennsylvania is one of the few states that (don't charge / aren't charged) sales tax on clothing.
3. A clearance sale (schedules / is scheduled) next week at this store.
4. All the staff members must (wear / be worn) uniforms at this store.

| Part 5 | Incomplete Sentences |

英文を完成させるのに最も適切な語句を（A）～（D）から選びましょう。

1. If you are not satisfied with the goods, the price ------- to you.
   (A) is refunding
   (B) has been refunded
   (C) will refund
   (D) will be refunded

2. We have ------- a voucher with this letter offering a 10% discount for your next purchase.
   (A) enclose
   (B) enclosed
   (C) been enclosed
   (D) enclosing

3. According to the e-mail from the shop, all fees are payable when the invoice ------- .
   (A) is issued
   (B) issues
   (C) is issuing
   (D) has issued

4. I'm pleased to announce that our end-of-season sale ------- record profits.
   (A) was generated
   (B) generated
   (C) has been generated
   (D) generating

5. During the clearance sale, the store ------- 5% for cash payment.
   (A) is discounted
   (B) has been discounted
   (C) discount
   (D) will discount

6. The new shopping mall ------- at a cost of approximately 10 million dollars.

(A) was constructed
(B) is constructing
(C) constructs
(D) will construct

7. The shop manager finally admitted an error in the bill and ------- to reduce the fee.

(A) was offered
(B) would be offered
(C) offering
(D) offered

Part 6 解法のコツ 〈定型表現 2〉

イベントの発表、告知などを扱った英文では、「～をお知らせいたします」や「～で開催されます」のような定型表現が数多く出てきます。こうした定型表現が語句挿入の問題に使われることもあるので、ぜひ慣れておきましょう。

Check

1～5 の英文中で下線を引いた語句とその日本語訳とを線で結びましょう。

1. We <u>are pleased to announce</u> the launch of our new brand.   •   • ～までに

2. Visitors <u>are encouraged to use</u> public transportation.   •   • ～にご参加ください

3. Applications must come in <u>no later than</u> May 31.   •   • 開催されます

4. The annual stockholders' meeting <u>takes place</u> next week.   •   • ～を発表いたします

5. <u>Please join us for</u> a complimentary online seminar.   •   • ～をご利用ください

Part 6 Text Completion

次の英文を読み、空所に入れるのに最も適切な語句や文を（A）～（D）から選びましょう。

Questions 8-11 refer to the following notice.

Garage sales: permit requirements

Under local government bylaw 2020-17, a permit is now required for anyone wishing to hold a garage or yard sale. This permit is available at a cost of $10 from the Inquiries desk at City Hall, or online using a credit card. ------- .
8.

All permit applications must be submitted at least 10 working days before the garage sale is due to take place. Any request for cancellation of a permit must be submitted no later than two working days before the date ------- the garage sale is due to take place.
9.

Notes:

· It ------- to advertise a garage sale with a sign other than at the same location.
10.

- Only one garage sale may be authorized per year for the same person and address, and the sale must be held at the address listed.
- No garage sale may last more than four consecutive days.
- No garage sale may be held at any time other than between 10:00 A.M. and 7:00 P.M.

The maximum --------- for conducting a sale without a license is $200.
_{11.}

8. (A) Please note that only cash is acceptable.
   (B) On the other hand, the permit is no longer necessary.
   (C) Click on this link and scroll down to "permit application."
   (D) The site has been discontinued recently.

9. (A) on which
   (B) where
   (C) which
   (D) in that

10. (A) forbids
    (B) is forbidden
    (C) is forbidding
    (D) will forbid

11. (A) wage
    (B) leeway
    (C) height
    (D) fine

Part 7　解法のコツ　〈複数文書問題 1〉

Part 7 の後半では、複数の文書が 1 セットになった問題が計 5 題出題されます。その内訳は次のようになっています。

名　称	形　式	出題数
ダブルパッセージ問題	2 つの文書を読み 5 つの設問に答える	2 題
トリプルパッセージ問題	3 つの文書を読み 5 つの設問に答える	3 題

Check

問題の指示文は次のようになっており、文書の形式がわかります。

Questions 176-180 refer to the following e-mail and schedule.
　　　　⇒ダブルパッセージ問題の例

Questions 196-200 refer to the following Web page and e-mails.
　　　　⇒トリプルパッセージ問題の例

いずれも難易度が高く、5 つの設問の中には必ず複数の文書の情報を組み合わせないと解けない問題が含まれています。ただし、それ以外の問題はシングルパッセージ問題と変わらないので、そうした問題から先に取り組むと良いでしょう。複数の文書の中で特定の文書に関する設問には、According to the e-mail（eメールによれば）や In the e-mail（eメールの中で）のような指示が含まれることもあります。

14. In the first Web site post, the word "imminent" in paragraph 1, line 1, is closest in meaning to

複数文書のうち、最初のウェブサイトへの投稿だけを読めば解ける問題です。

次の英文を読み、設問に対する答えとして最も適切なものを（A）〜（D）から選びましょう。

Questions 12-16 refer to the following Web site announcement and comments.

---

https://www.renniesartsandcrafts.com

Rennies Arts & Crafts

Posted August 25, 4:20 P.M.

With great regret we have to announce the imminent closure of Rennies Arts & Crafts. Our final day will be Saturday 27 of August. The escalated move to online buying has been a major factor, but the decision by Cleveland city council to fully pedestrianize Bold Street has proved to be the final straw.

We have been trading on Bold Street for 42 years, so closing is a huge disappointment. We pride ourselves on our service and would like to thank our tremendous staff, past and present, for their support. Finally, a very big thank you to all our loyal customers who have become friends over the years.

....

Posted August 26, 3:17 P.M.

We would like to thank you all for your kind messages regarding the closure of Rennies Arts & Crafts. Many have asked about our online business, and it will also be permanently closed shortly. Once again, we would like to thank all of our customers for their support over the last 42 years. You will be missed.

| Home | New Items | Comments | Contact Us |

 Patricia Cromwell ★ ★ ★ ★ ★

I visited the store with my mother on its final day. She was a regular customer for more than 30 years, and I bought Christmas presents there many times. We were shocked at the news of its closure, so we wanted to say thank you in person to the manager, Kate. She was always kind and helpful. We really miss you, Kate!

12. What is the purpose of the first Web site post?

    (A) To advertise a new business
    (B) To announce the closure of a store
    (C) To report the decision by a city council
    (D) To apologize for the delay

13. In the first Web site post, the word "imminent" in paragraph 1, line 1, is closest in meaning to

    (A) complete
    (B) voluntary
    (C) impending
    (D) avoidable

14. What is indicated about Rennies Arts & Crafts?

    (A) The store is located on Bold Street.
    (B) The store will be closed on Sunday.
    (C) It has been in business for almost 40 years.
    (D) It will continue its online business.

15. According to the comment, who is Kate?

    (A) A regular customer
    (B) The store manager
    (C) Patricia's daughter
    (D) Patricia's mother

16. When did Ms. Cromwell visit the store?

    (A) On August 25
    (B) On August 26
    (C) On August 27
    (D) On August 28

Communicative Training

Part 7 で取り上げたウェブサイトでのお知らせとコメントを使ってパートナーと英語で互いに質問をしてみましょう。答える際は、"Yes." や "No." だけで終わらないよう適宜、情報を追加しましょう。

Student A
Student B（パートナー）に下記の質問をしてみましょう。

Student B
Student A（パートナー）の質問に対して Part 7 の英文を見ながら答えましょう。

1. When will Rennies Arts & Crafts be closed?

2. What street is the store located on?

3. Is the store going to continue its online business?

4. Is Patricia the manager of the store?

5. (You choose!)

UNIT 06 Finances

Vocabulary

1. 1～10の語句の意味として適切なものをa～jの中から選びましょう。　CD 1-72

1. property	＿＿＿＿	a．強調する
2. raise	＿＿＿＿	b．年金
3. contribution	＿＿＿＿	c．退職する
4. resolution	＿＿＿＿	d．昇給
5. emphasize	＿＿＿＿	e．違反、不履行
6. retire	＿＿＿＿	f．緊急性
7. urgency	＿＿＿＿	g．不動産、財産
8. pension	＿＿＿＿	h．解決
9. invest	＿＿＿＿	i．投資する
10. breach	＿＿＿＿	j．積立金、貢献

2. 語群の中から適切な日本語訳を選び、派生語の図を完成させましょう。

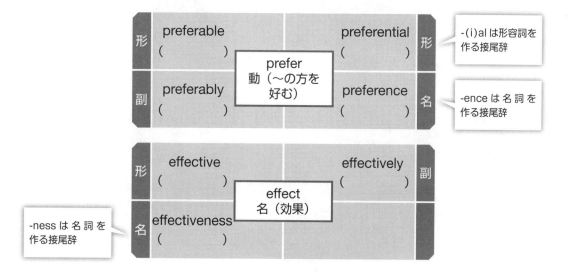

形	preferable （　　　　）	preferential （　　　　）	形
	prefer 動（～の方を好む）		
副	preferably （　　　　）	preference （　　　　）	名

-(i)al は形容詞を作る接尾辞

-ence は名詞を作る接尾辞

形	effective （　　　　）	effectively （　　　　）	副
	effect 名（効果）		
名	effectiveness （　　　　）		

-ness は名詞を作る接尾辞

望ましくは、できれば	より望ましい	好み	優先的な
効果的に	効果的な	有効性	

Part 1　解法のコツ　〈様々な主語〉

複数の人物が写っている写真の場合、選択肢の主語がすべて異なる場合があります。それぞれの主語を聞き漏らさないよう、冒頭の主語に注意を払いましょう。

👆 Check

下の写真の描写として最も適切な英文を 1 〜 4 の中から選びましょう。

1. They are queuing up to use an ATM.
2. The ATM is out of order.
3. The woman is opening her purse.
4. One of the men is paying at the cash register.

Part 1　Photographs

🎧 1-73, 74

(A)〜(D) の英文を聞き、写真を最も適切に描写しているものを選びましょう。

1.

(A)　　(B)　　(C)　　(D)

Part 2 　Question-Response

🎵 1-75～79

最初に聞こえてくる英文に対する応答として最も適切なものを（A）～（C）から選びましょう。

2. Mark your answer. 　　(A)　　　　(B)　　　　(C)
3. Mark your answer. 　　(A)　　　　(B)　　　　(C)
4. Mark your answer. 　　(A)　　　　(B)　　　　(C)
5. Mark your answer. 　　(A)　　　　(B)　　　　(C)

Part 3 　Conversations

🎵 1-80～82

会話を聞き、6 ～ 8 の設問に対する解答として最も適切なものを（A）～（D）から選びましょう。

Type	Your contributions/funds are …
Plan A	managed exclusively by our team.
Plan B	jointly managed with an advisor from our team.
Plan C	entirely self-managed.
Plan D	converted to foreign exchange.

6. Look at the graphic. Which plan will the man most likely choose?

   (A) Plan A
   (B) Plan B
   (C) Plan C
   (D) Plan D

7. What does the woman ask the man?

   (A) Whether he wants to join her team or not
   (B) His experience in investment
   (C) When he plans to retire
   (D) How much he plans to invest

8. What does the man mean when he says, "maybe I'm not being realistic"?

   (A) He has no plan to retire.
   (B) He has already retired.
   (C) He wants to retire as soon as possible.
   (D) He probably won't be able to retire at 60.

Part 4 **Talks** 1-83〜85

トークを聞き、9〜11の設問に対する解答として最も適切なものを（A）〜（D）から選びましょう。

9. Who most likely is listening to this message?

(A) A magazine subscriber
(B) A charge card holder
(C) A check holder
(D) An employee of a credit card company

10. What is the listener instructed to do in order to request a new PIN?

(A) Press 1
(B) Press 2
(C) Press 3
(D) Press 4

11. Which of the following is only available between 8:00 A.M. and 9:00 P.M.?

(A) Point redemption
(B) Application for a cash advance
(C) Account balance inquiries
(D) Campaign registration

Communicative Training

1. Part 2 のスクリプトにある最初の問いかけを使ってパートナーと英語で互いに質問をしてみましょう。質問に答える際は、下の回答例を参考にしましょう。なお、スクリプトは教員から配布されます。

Student A
Student B（パートナー）に Part 2 のスクリプトにある最初の問いかけをしてみましょう。

Student B
Student A（パートナー）の質問に対して下の回答例を参考に答えましょう。

Q2
・すみません、小切手は受け付けておりません。
・少々お待ちください。マネージャーに確認します。
・（You choose!)

Q3
・はい、とても嬉しいです。
・えっ、どうして知っているのですか？
・（You choose!)

Q4
・はい、彼はとても信頼できます。
・はい、彼とは知り合って 10年になります。
・（You choose!)

Q5
・えっ、本当ですか？　それは素晴らしいニュースですね。
・いいえ、しませんでした。誰がそんなことを言ったのですか？
・（You choose!)

2. Part 3 の対話スクリプトの内容について、パートナーと英語で互いに質問をしてみましょう。質問に答える際は、対話スクリプトだけを見るようにし、下の質問は見ないようにしましょう。なお、スクリプトは教員から配布されます。

Student A
Student B（パートナー）に下記の質問をしてみましょう。

Student B
Student A（パートナー）の質問に対して Part 3 の対話スクリプトを見ながら答えましょう。

1. Does the man want to stop investing in a managed private fund?
2. What does he find too stressful?
3. According to the woman, in what area is her company the market leader?
4. At what age does the man want to retire?
5. (You choose!)

Reading Section

選択肢に目を通し、(high / large / heavy / strong) のように、同じ品詞の単語が並んでいる場合は、語彙の知識を問う「語彙問題」です。語彙問題も品詞問題と同様によく出題されますが、① borrow と lend、rent のように、意味の似た単語、② purse と purser、pursuit のように形の似た単語という2つのパターンがあるので注意しておきましょう。

Check

1〜4の英文中のカッコ内から正しい語を選び○で囲みましょう。

1. A lot of banks are unwilling to (borrow / lend / rent) money to new businesses.
2. I took a coin out of my (purse / purser / pursuit) and gave it to the child.
3. Rita is a financial adviser and advises people where to (invest / inquire / inhibit) their money.
4. We can expect a substantial pay raise as well as a (many / large / heavy) bonus this year.

Part 5   Incomplete Sentences

英文を完成させるのに最も適切な語句を（A）〜（D）から選びましょう。

1. People who work in banks know a lot about ------- and accounting.

   (A) defiance
   (B) finance
   (C) fragrance
   (D) fiancé

2. Benefits offered by companies can vary widely, which is why it's important to ------- the benefits packages being offered.

   (A) demonstrate
   (B) discard
   (C) prepare
   (D) compare

3. If you're thinking about buying your first home, please join us for a ------- homebuyer seminar hosted by Best Rate Mortgage.

   (A) documentary
   (B) fragmentary
   (C) complimentary
   (D) parliamentary

4. City Union Bank is ------- looking for an accounting manager to work at our new branch in Perth.

   (A) currently
   (B) anciently
   (C) absently
   (D) leniently

5. The financial adviser emphasized that employees may opt out of the company's ------- plan.

   (A) tension
   (B) omission
   (C) invasion
   (D) pension

6. Those employees ------- by changes to the company's health plan are advised to watch the online seminar.

   (A) affected
   (B) effected
   (C) objected
   (D) defected

7. The compensation package will include both a(n) ------- salary and employee benefits.

(A) gradual
(B) mutual
(C) annual
(D) ritual

文挿入問題は、段落の最後に空欄が設定されている場合と段落中に空欄が設定されている場合があります。段落の最後に空欄が設定されている場合は直前の文にうまくつながるかを確認すれば良いだけですが、段落中に空欄が設定されている場合は直前の文だけでなく、直後の文にうまくつながるかも忘れずに確認しましょう。

We can never thank Oliver enough for being at our side from the beginning to the end in the purchase of our Gold Coast apartment. -------. But he was always there to find a solution ....
10.

直前だけでなく、直後の文にうまくつながるかにも注意しましょう！

Part 6 Text Completion

次の英文を読み、空所に入れるのに最も適切な語句や文を（A）～（D）から選びましょう。

Questions 8-11 refer to the following Web site.

Moneywise — The right choice for the right property

Moneywise is an independent brokerage company with several agencies throughout Queensland. ------- a real estate broker, our mission is to assist
8.
our clients in ------- real estate projects (purchase of a primary or secondary
9.
residence, rental property, etc.) by providing them with banking expertise, saving them time and optimizing the banking conditions of their loans (rates, monthly payments, guarantees).

Moneywise customer reviews — Read our clients' testimonials

"We can never thank Oliver enough for being at our side from the beginning to the end in the purchase of our Gold Coast apartment. -------. But he was
10.
always there to find a solution, answering our questions, calming our anxieties, always being positive, dynamic, smiling and -------. Once again, a
11.
big thank you to Oliver and the Moneywise team, whom we highly recommend." (Gordon & Lou Macari, Tamborine Mountain)

8. (A) As
   (B) For
   (C) In
   (D) With

9. (A) your
   (B) its
   (C) our
   (D) their

10. (A) With his conscientious support and help, everything went very smoothly.
    (B) During the three months that we were working together, there were ups and downs.
    (C) We really got a good deal on the apartment.
    (D) We're terribly sorry to hear that he finally left Moneywise.

11. (A) informedly
    (B) inform
    (C) informative
    (D) information

| Part 7 | 解法のコツ | 〈手紙書式〉 |

eメールと並び、手紙もよく出題される文書形式の１つです。eメールと似ていますが、レターヘッドからeメールよりも多くの情報を得ることができます。次の書式例で特徴に慣れておきましょう。

手紙の書式例

UNC Financial Corporation

1010 GRAND AVE
KANSAS CITY, MO
64106

Ms. Hannah Hoffman
511 Delaware St Suite
200, Kansas City, MO
64105

July 13

Dear Ms. Hoffman,
_____
_____
_____

Sincerely,

Anthony Dawson

Anthony Dawson
Manager
UNC Financial
Corporation

Enclosure

■レターヘッド
差出人の会社名、住所、電話番号などが記されます。

■宛先の氏名・住所
宛先の氏名、住所が記されます。

■日付

■本文
最初に、宛名が記されます。
次に、用件が述べられますが、多くの場合、「導入⇒本論⇒結論」という流れになります。

結びは、(Yours) Sincerely のほか、(Best) Regards などもよく使われます。

■差出人の署名等
差出人の署名、氏名、所属（役職、部署、会社名など）が記されます。

■同封物の有無

次の英文を読み、設問に対する答えとして最も適切なものを（A）〜（D）から選びましょう。

Questions 12-15 refer to the following letter.

Sammy Silkman

45, Lime Street,
Maccletown, SK103AQ

September 20, 2023
Mr. Owen Meany
Lucre Hall, Cheshire, CH1 1XX
Ref: Delayed Salary Payments

Dear Mr. Meany,

I am writing this letter in the hope of obtaining a quick resolution to the non-payment of players' salaries. — [1] —. These salaries are already two months in arrears and non-payment represents a breach of the Professional League's Code of Conduct, which guarantees the prompt payment of salaries. This situation is having a damaging effect on team morale. — [2] —.

I have already discussed this matter with you in person, but action has yet to be taken. I am submitting this official written request in the hope that it will communicate the seriousness of the situation to you. Failure to comply with our request will leave us with no other option than to pursue legal action. — [3] —.

I appreciate that you have been making efforts to maintain the financial stability of the club. However, we wish the urgency of our claims to be recognized and honored at your earliest opportunity. — [4] —.

Sincerely,

Sammy Silkman

Sammy Silkman
Representative, Players Union

12. What is the purpose of the letter?

   (A) To schedule a meeting
   (B) To ask for a legal action
   (C) To adopt a resolution
   (D) To claim payment

13. The word "breach" in paragraph 1, line 3, is closest in meaning to

   (A) violation
   (B) obedience
   (C) consensus
   (D) view

14. What is indicated about the salaries?

(A) They haven't been increased at all.
(B) They have been only partially paid.
(C) They haven't been paid for two months.
(D) They have been reduced without notice.

15. In which of the positions marked [1], [2], [3], and [4] does the following sentence best belong?
"In addition, it is causing considerable mental duress to the players and their families, too."

(A) [1]
(B) [2]
(C) [3]
(D) [4]

Communicative Training

Part 7 で取り上げた手紙を使ってパートナーと英語で互いに質問をしてみましょう。答える際は、"Yes." や "No." だけで終わらないよう適宜、情報を追加しましょう。

Student A
Student B（パートナー）に下記の質問をしてみましょう。

Student B
Student A（パートナー）の質問に対して Part 7 の英文を見ながら答えましょう。

1. Who is Sammy Silkman?
2. What does he say about players' salaries?
3. According to him, what does the Professional League's Code of Conduct guarantee?
4. Has he discussed the matter with Mr. Meany in person yet?
5. (You choose!)

UNIT 07 Transportation

ABCD Vocabulary

1．1〜10 の語句の意味として適切なものを a〜j の中から選びましょう。　CD 1-86

1. customs	＿＿＿＿	a．税関
2. belongings	＿＿＿＿	b．葬式、葬儀
3. alternative	＿＿＿＿	c．礼儀正しい
4. suspend	＿＿＿＿	d．スリ、スリを働く
5. funeral	＿＿＿＿	e．通勤する、通学する
6. alert	＿＿＿＿	f．所持品、所有物
7. departure	＿＿＿＿	g．一時停止する、一時中断する
8. courteous	＿＿＿＿	h．警戒して
9. commute	＿＿＿＿	i．代わりの
10. pickpocket	＿＿＿＿	j．出発

2．語群の中から適切な日本語訳を選び、派生語の図を完成させましょう。

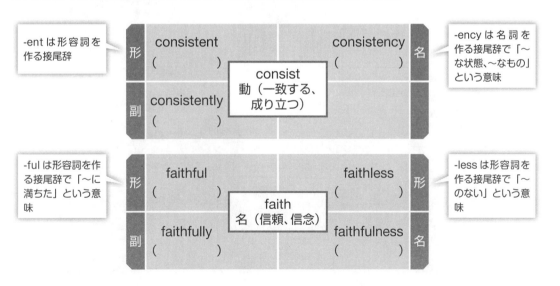

-ent は形容詞を作る接尾辞

| 形 | consistent （　　　） | consistency （　　　） | 名 |

-ency は名詞を作る接尾辞で「〜な状態、〜なもの」という意味

consist
動（一致する、成り立つ）

| 副 | consistently （　　　） |

-ful は形容詞を作る接尾辞で「〜に満ちた」という意味

| 形 | faithful （　　　） | faithless （　　　） | 形 |

faith
名（信頼、信念）

-less は形容詞を作る接尾辞で「〜のない」という意味

| 副 | faithfully （　　　） | faithfulness （　　　） | 名 |

矛盾なく　（言行などが）一貫して　（言行などの）一貫性
不誠実な　誠実な　誠実に　誠実さ

73

Listening Section

Part 1 解法のコツ　〈現在完了形〉

写真描写問題では、「～している」という現在進行形が中心ですが、「～してしまった」のような現在完了形が使われることもあります。〈have / has+ 過去分詞〉の部分を聞き逃さないようにしましょう。

Check

下の写真の描写として最も適切な英文を 1 ～ 4 の中から選びましょう。

1. Some suitcases have been stacked on the floor.
2. Some suitcases have been left on a baggage conveyor belt.
3. Passengers are pulling their suitcases behind them.
4. Passengers are putting their suitcases on the cart.

Part 1 **Photographs**　　　　1-87, 88

（A）～（D）の英文を聞き、写真を最も適切に描写しているものを選びましょう。

1.

(A)　　(B)　　(C)　　(D)

Part 2 Question-Response

CD 1-89～93

最初に聞こえてくる英文に対する応答として最も適切なものを（A）～（C）から選びましょう。

2. Mark your answer.　　(A)　　(B)　　(C)
3. Mark your answer.　　(A)　　(B)　　(C)
4. Mark your answer.　　(A)　　(B)　　(C)
5. Mark your answer.　　(A)　　(B)　　(C)

Part 3 Conversations

 1-94～96

会話を聞き、6～8の設問に対する解答として最も適切なものを（A）～（D）から選びましょう。

6. Where is the conversation taking place?

(A) At a hotel
(B) At an airport
(C) At a bus terminal
(D) At a taxi stand

7. What does the woman say to the man?

(A) They have two options to choose from.
(B) Local buses are more frequent.
(C) It's difficult to get a taxi at this hour.
(D) It takes 10 minutes to walk to the bus stop.

8. What does the woman suggest they do?

(A) Take the shuttle bus
(B) Take a taxi
(C) Rent a car
(D) Walk to the bus stop

交通機関に関するアナウンスには、下記のような基本的な流れがあるので、情報がどのような順序で出てくるか予測することができます。慣れておきましょう。

1. 呼びかけ	May I have your attention, please?
2. 目的	Due to damage caused by heavy rain on the tracks, the train service to Chicago has been suspended.
	⇒電車の運行停止のお知らせ
3. 追加情報、注意事項	If you have tickets to Chicago for today, you can take advantage of our emergency bus service.
	⇒代替措置のお知らせ
4. 結び	We apologize for any inconvenience this may cause.
	⇒お詫び

Part 4　Talks　　　　　　　　　　　　　　　　　　　🎧 1-97〜99

トークを聞き、9〜11 の設問に対する解答として最も適切なものを（A)〜(D）から選びましょう。

9. Where would this announcement be heard?

(A) On an airplane
(B) At an airport terminal
(C) On a shuttle bus
(D) At an aircraft factory

10. According to the speaker, what is indicated about the flight?

(A) It departed as scheduled.
(B) Its departure was delayed for 15 minutes.
(C) It is arriving as scheduled.
(D) It arrived 15 minutes late.

11. What are listeners asked NOT to do?

(A) Open the overhead lockers
(B) Release their seat belt now
(C) Check their personal belongings
(D) Follow the blue signs

Communicative Training

1. Part 2 のスクリプトにある最初の問いかけを使ってパートナーと英語で互いに質問をしてみましょう。質問に答える際は、下の回答例を参考にしましょう。なお、スクリプトは教員から配布されます。

Student A
Student B（パートナー）に Part 2 のスクリプトにある最初の問いかけをしてみましょう。

Student B
Student A（パートナー）の質問に対して下の回答例を参考に答えましょう。

Q2
・もちろんです。実は、あなたにそうしてもらおうとお願いするところでした。
・すみません。窓側の席*が好きなのです。
　　　　　　　　　　　　　　*a window seat
・(You choose!)

Q3
・ええ、構いませんよ。
・そうできたらいいのですが（できません）。
・(You choose!)

Q4
・それは良い考えですね。
・あまり遠くないから歩きませんか？
・(You choose!)

Q5
・もちろんです。喜んでさせていただきます。
・すみません、これから歯科に行かないといけないのです。
・(You choose!)

2. Part 3 の対話スクリプトの内容について、パートナーと英語で互いに質問をしてみましょう。質問に答える際は、対話スクリプトだけを見るようにし、下の質問は見ないようにしましょう。なお、スクリプトは教員から配布されます。

Student A
Student B（パートナー）に下記の質問をしてみましょう。

Student B
Student A（パートナー）の質問に対して Part 3 の対話スクリプトを見ながら答えましょう。

1. Do they want to go to the airport or the hotel?
2. According to the woman, how many choices do they have?
3. What are they*?
4. What does the man say would be most convenient?
5. (You choose!)
*they = the choices

Reading Section

Part 5　解法のコツ　〈代名詞問題 1〉

選択肢に代名詞が並んでいる場合は、その代名詞が指す名詞が①単数か複数か？　②人かどうか？
の 2 点に注意しましょう。また、下の表（一人称の代名詞）を参考にして人称代名詞・所有代名詞・
再帰代名詞の働きについても確認しておきましょう。

数	人称代名詞			所有代名詞 *「〜のもの」という意味を表します。	再帰代名詞 *「〜自身」という意味を表します。
	主格 *主語として使われます。	所有格 *「〜の」という意味を表します。	目的格 *目的語として使われます。		
単数形	I	my	me	mine	myself
複数形	we	our	us	ours	ourselves

Check

1 〜 4 の英文中のカッコ内から正しい語を選び○で囲みましょう。

1. Our city prides (it / its / itself) on great public transportation.
2. Volunteers for the charity event must provide (they / their / them) own transportation.
3. All of (we / our / us) were asked to answer the survey.
4. Jeff commutes to work by train, but he's planning to buy a car of (he / his / himself) own.

Part 5　Incomplete Sentences

英文を完成させるのに最も適切な語句を（A）〜（D）から選びましょう。

1. According to the survey, the main reason students drive to campus is because ------- offers the shortest commuting time.

   (A) they
   (B) its
   (C) it
   (D) themselves

2. The heavy traffic delayed ------- for over an hour, so we missed our flight.

   (A) we
   (B) our
   (C) us
   (D) ourselves

3. In Los Angeles many companies encourage ------- employees to use alternative means of transportation, rather than cars.

   (A) it
   (B) them
   (C) its
   (D) their

4. Arthur says that he can't help but talk to ------- while driving to work.

   (A) he
   (B) himself
   (C) his
   (D) they

5. We were wondering if you could give ------- a ride to the nearest station.

    (A) ourselves
    (B) us
    (C) we
    (D) ours

6. The presenter claimed that as a commuter service, the ferry has outlived ------- usefulness.

    (A) it
    (B) him
    (C) its
    (D) his

7. I offered to pay the cost of the taxi, but he insisted that ------- would pay.

    (A) he
    (B) ourselves
    (C) me
    (D) I

Part 6 解法のコツ 〈定型表現 3〉

注意喚起の案内などを扱った英文では、「お気をつけください」や「ご協力のほど、よろしくお願い申し上げます」のような定型表現が数多く登場します。こうした定型表現が語句挿入の問題に使われることもあるので、ぜひ慣れておきましょう。

☞ Check

1～5の英文中で下線を引いた語句とその日本語訳を線で結びましょう。

1. <u>Please be informed that</u> on Tuesday, November 7 there will be a scheduled power outage.   •

    • ご迷惑

2. Thank you for your <u>patience</u> and understanding.   •

    • ～をお知らせします

3. <u>Watch your step.</u>   •

    • 足元にご注意ください

4. We apologize for any <u>inconvenience</u> this may cause.   •

    • ご辛抱

5. <u>Beware of theft.</u>   •

    • 盗難にご注意ください

Part 6   Text Completion

次の英文を読み、空所に入れるのに最も適切な語句や文を（A）～（D）から選びましょう。

Questions 8-11 refer to the following notice.

Travel Advice on Paris Metro

In recent years, the incidence of pickpocketing and theft on the Paris Metro has risen dramatically, and tourists in particular need to be extra ------- . In order to minimize your personal risk, please follow the following pieces of advice:

1. Avoid ------- a backpack, or carry it in front of you. Shoulder bags or
   _{9.} fanny packs are safer options.
2. Keep your wallet in an inside pocket, or in a pocket with a zipper.
3. Never take your eyes off your luggage and be alert to all and any
   unusual situations.
4. Try not to look like a tourist in your dress and behavior.
5. Carry only the minimum amount of cash and never display valuables or
   money in plain sight.

------- . They try to blend in with the crowd, so ------- appearance may be that
_{10.}   _{11.}
of a tourist, especially in very touristy or busy places. Stay alert, stay safe.

8. (A) incautious
(B) negligent
(C) sloppy
(D) vigilant

9. (A) use
(B) using
(C) to use
(D) having used

10. (A) Have you ever got lost while traveling?
(B) Don't forget that pickpockets really stand out!
(C) Remember, pickpockets don't always look like thieves!
(D) Never forget these pieces of advice.

11. (A) their
(B) your
(C) our
(D) its

Part 7　解法のコツ　〈クロスレファレンス問題〉

複数文書問題では、2つの文書を読まないと解けない形式の問題（クロスレファレンス問題）が必ず含まれます。次の例では、文書Aで会議の開始時間を読み取り、文書Bでスミス氏が30分遅れることを読み取って初めて正解の（D）にたどり着けます。慣れるまでは難しいですが、問題を数多くこなしながらコツを掴みましょう。

What time will Mr. Smith attend the meeting?
(A) 2:00
(B) 2:30
(C) 3:00
(D) 3:30

文書A

The meeting starts at 3 P.M.

会議は午後3時に開始

文書B

I'll arrive 30 minutes late. Sorry.

John Smith

スミス氏は30分遅刻する

スミス氏の会議到着時間は午後3:30

次の英文を読み、設問に対する答えとして最も適切なものを（A）～（D）から選びましょう。

Questions 12-16 refer to the following advertisement, form and e-mail.

Bostock's Luxury Buses

With more than 55 years of experience in a highly competitive market, we distinguish ourselves by our attention to detail, promising travelers an unforgettable travel experience. For our customers, it means the feeling of being taken care of by competent and professional people who spare no effort to ensure their safety, comfort and satisfaction. Our courteous and professional drivers are trained to help you enjoy your journey, and we pride ourselves on the quality of our fleet, our punctuality and professionalism.

Executive vehicle with 6 to 8 seats

Rent a luxury station wagon or SUV with driver in small groups for your trips to hotels, airports, and train stations.

Executive minibus with 15 to 20 seats

Larger than the van but smaller than the bus. Ideal for city travel and can be used anywhere thanks to its small size.

Intermediate economy bus (20 to 35 passengers) / Adapted economy bus (20 to 30 passengers)

Ideal for seminars and school trips. It is also often requested for family occasions such as weddings, funerals, etc. It's also suitable for customers with a limited budget. The adapted buses have been designed with a reduced-mobility clientele in mind.

Luxury Bus (35 to 50 passengers)

Ideal for very long trips or important events as they allow a large number of people to be accommodated in one coach.

Service Inquiry Form

Name	Robert	Ironside
	First Name	Last Name

E-mail | rironside@cmail.com

Subject | A few questions

Details | Hi. I'm interested in booking a bus for a family wedding. Our group of 19 includes one wheelchair user. Would this require the use of the Adapted Economy Bus? Or would it be possible to fit everyone into the executive minibus? If possible, I'd prefer a smaller vehicle. Also, does the Intermediate Economy Bus have a toilet on board?

Submit

To: Robert Ironside <rironside@cmail.com>

From: Gerry Daly <g.daly@bostocks-luxury-buses.com>

Date: October 18

Subject: Re: A few questions

Dear Mr. Ironside,

Many thanks for considering using our bus service. I'm pleased to inform you that we have recently upgraded our executive minibus and it can now accommodate up to 20 passengers, including two wheelchair users. With regard to the on-board toilet, regrettably, these are only available on the larger buses with a capacity up to 50.

Please feel free to contact us again through our online booking form for a quote, or through this inquiry form if you have any more questions.

Sincerely,

Gerry Daly
Bostock's Luxury Buses

---

12. For whom is the advertisement most likely intended?

(A) People who want to become bus drivers

(B) People who want to become travel agents

(C) People interested in chartering a bus

(D) People interested in overseas travel

13. In the advertisement, what is indicated about the vehicles?

(A) Seating capacity

(B) Storage space

(C) Available dates

(D) Rental rates

14. In the e-mail, the word "quote" in paragraph 2, line 2, is closest in meaning to

(A) survey
(B) feedback
(C) estimate
(D) reservation

15. What type of vehicle will Mr. Ironside most likely select after he's read the e-mail?

(A) An executive vehicle
(B) An executive minibus
(C) An intermediate economy bus
(D) An adapted economy bus

16. What type of vehicle has a toilet on board?

(A) An executive minibus
(B) An intermediate economy bus
(C) An adapted economy bus
(D) A luxury bus

Communicative Training

Part 7 で取り上げたフォームと e メールを使ってパートナーと英語で互いに質問をしてみましょう。答える際は、"Yes." や "No." だけで終わらないよう適宜、情報を追加しましょう。

Student A
Student B（パートナー）に下記の質問をしてみましょう。

Student B
Student A（パートナー）の質問に対して Part 7 の英文を見ながら答えましょう。

1. What is Mr. Ironside interested in booking a bus for?
2. How many people are there in his party?
3. Who replied to the e-mail from Mr. Ironside?
4. Does the intermediate economy bus have a toilet on board?
5.（You choose!）

航空機（の利用）に関連した重要語句一覧

出発　departure

航空会社 airline	預け入れ荷物 check-in baggage
航空券 airplane ticket	機内持ち込み手荷物 carry-on baggage
搭乗券 boarding pass	超過手荷物 excess baggage
パスポート passport	保安検査（場） security check
チェックインカウンター check-in counter	乗り継ぎカウンター connecting flight counter

到着　arrival

入国カード landing card	目的地 destination
入国管理（所） immigration	国内便 domestic flight
税関 customs	国際便 international flight
税関申告書 customs declaration form	直行便 direct flight
手荷物受取所 baggage claim area	乗継便 connecting flight

UNIT 08 Technology

AB CD Vocabulary

1. 1 ～ 10 の語句の意味として適切なものを a ～ j の中から選びましょう。　🎧 2-01

1. emission	_____	a . 再生可能な
2. registration	_____	b . 超高層ビル
3. subscription	_____	c . 登録
4. finalize	_____	d . 誓約、公約
5. innovation	_____	e . 発売、公開
6. renewable	_____	f . 最新式の、最先端の
7. state-of-the-art	_____	g . ～を完成させる
8. commitment	_____	h . 革新
9. release	_____	i . 会費、予約購読
10. skyscraper	_____	j . 排出（物）、放出（物）

2．語群の中から適切な日本語訳を選び、派生語の図を完成させましょう。

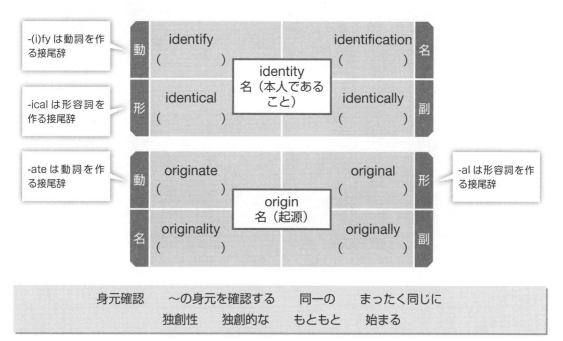

身元確認　～の身元を確認する　同一の　まったく同じに
独創性　独創的な　もともと　始まる

Listening Section

Part 1 解法のコツ 〈風景の描写〉

風景写真の場合、まずどのような場所かを把握しましょう。また、人物写真の場合と違い、選択肢の主語がすべて異なることも多いので、写真と照合しながら聞き取りましょう。また、人がいないことを示す unoccupied や empty などの表現にも慣れておきましょう。

Benches are unoccupied.
（ベンチは空いています）

Houses line the street.
（家が通りに建ち並んでいます）

The road is empty.
（道路には人けがありません）

Part 1 Photographs

CD 2-02, 03

(A)〜(D) の英文を聞き、写真を最も適切に描写しているものを選びましょう。

1.

(A)　　(B)　　(C)　　(D)

最初に聞こえてくる文は疑問文がほとんどですが、中には平叙文もあります。例えば、問題点を指摘することで、解決策や援助を求めるというように、何かを伝えて相手の応答を期待するタイプです。いろんなパターンがありますので、少しずつ慣れましょう。

問いかけ	Oh, no! The printer is jammed again.
正解の応答例	We need to buy a new one.

Part 2 Question-Response

 2-04～08

最初に聞こえてくる英文に対する応答として最も適切なものを（A）～（C）から選びましょう。

2. Mark your answer.   (A)   (B)   (C)
3. Mark your answer.   (A)   (B)   (C)
4. Mark your answer.   (A)   (B)   (C)
5. Mark your answer.   (A)   (B)   (C)

Part 3 解法のコツ   〈話題を問う設問〉

会話の話題を問う設問では、"What is the conversation mainly about?" や "What are the speakers discussing?" のように、何について話しているかをストレートに問うものが中心となります。しかし、この他にも "What is the problem?" や "What is wrong with the project?" のように、話題となっている問題点を具体的に問う形式もありますので慣れておきましょう。

- What is the conversation mainly about?
- What are the speakers discussing?

「何についての会話ですか？」

- What is wrong with the project?
- According to the man, what is the problem?

「（話題となっている）問題点は何ですか？」

Part 3 Conversations

2-09～11

会話を聞き、6 ～ 8 の設問に対する解答として最も適切なものを（A）～（D）から選びましょう。

6. What are the speakers discussing?

(A) A user's manual
(B) A software product
(C) The release date of a product
(D) A new store

7. What does the woman ask the man?

(A) What he is working on right now
(B) How he created the app
(C) What release notes are
(D) Whether he has heard of release notes

8. When will the man finish the job he's working on now?

(A) Tonight
(B) Tomorrow
(C) In two days
(D) In a week

ラジオ放送には、下記のような基本的な流れがあるので、情報がどのような順序で出てくるか予測することができます。慣れておきましょう。

1. 挨拶、番組紹介	You're listening to the morning show on Radio WACC.	

1. 挨拶、番組紹介　You're listening to the morning show on Radio WACC.
　⇒ラジオ局、番組名などの紹介

2. 目的　Let's hear the news for this weekend. We have the annual big event of the summer, the Bristol Technology Festival.
　⇒イベントのお知らせ

3. 詳細　Tickets are free but are required for entry. Pick up your tickets at City Hall or the city library by Friday.
　⇒チケットの料金や入手方法の連絡

4. 次の情報の紹介　Now, here's Susan Gilbert with our weekend weather report.
　⇒次は天気予報

🎧 2-12〜14

トークを聞き、9〜11の設問に対する解答として最も適切なものを（A）〜（D）から選びましょう。

9. What most likely is Dansk?

(A) A shipbuilding company
(B) A container leasing company
(C) A transport company
(D) A robotics company

10. According to the speaker, what is Dansk committed to?

(A) Using renewable energy and green fuel
(B) Producing robotically controlled ships
(C) Developing alternative energy
(D) Increasing their carbon footprint

11. What will you most likely hear after this talk?

(A) A weather report
(B) A traffic report
(C) A music program
(D) Entertainment news

Communicative Training

1. Part 2のスクリプトにある最初の問いかけを使ってパートナーと英語で互いに質問をしてみましょう。質問に答える際は、下の回答例を参考にしましょう。なお、スクリプトは教員から配布されます。

Student A
Student B（パートナー）にPart 2のスクリプトにある最初の問いかけをしてみましょう。

Student B
Student A（パートナー）の質問に対して下の回答例を参考に答えましょう。

Q2
・わかりました。私が見てあげましょう。
・それはいけませんね。最近パスワードを変えましたか？
・（You choose!）

Q3
・仕方ありませんね。
・それじゃ、どこか他のところに行きましょう。
・（You choose!）

Q4
・確かですか？　私はそうは思いません。
・その通りです。私たちはもっと時間が必要です。
・（You choose!）

Q5
・ええ、私もそのモデルがほしいです。
・ええ、彼が先週買ったと言っていました。
・（You choose!）

2. Part 3の対話スクリプトの内容について、パートナーと英語で互いに質問をしてみましょう。質問に答える際は、対話スクリプトだけを見るようにし、下の質問は見ないようにしましょう。なお、スクリプトは教員から配布されます。

Student A
Student B（パートナー）に下記の質問をしてみましょう。

Student B
Student A（パートナー）の質問に対してPart 3の対話スクリプトを見ながら答えましょう。

1. Who is working on the release notes, the man or the woman?
2. Is the woman familiar with release notes?
3. According to the man, what are release notes like?
4. When is he going to finish them?
5. (You choose!)

Reading Section

前置詞は名詞・代名詞の前に置かれて、〈前置詞＋（代）名詞〉の形で形容詞や副詞の働きをするので、選択肢に前置詞が並んでいる前置詞問題では、まず空所の直後にある（代）名詞に着目しましょう。また、rely on（〜に頼る）や aware of（〜に気づいて）のように、動詞や形容詞とセットになって決まった意味を表す表現も出題されるので、空所の直前にも注意を払いましょう。

Check

1〜4の英文中のカッコ内から正しい語を選び○で囲みましょう。

1. Admission to the event was limited (to / at / on) 300 participants.

2. We find it difficult to keep up (to / with / for) recent technological advances.

3. Our latest smartwatch sold out (in / at / on) the first week after its release.

4. The company attributes its success (for / to / on) the introduction of a new wireless service.

Part 5　Incomplete Sentences

英文を完成させるのに最も適切な語句を（A)〜(D）から選びましょう。

1. They told us that the new plant would be completed ------- the end of September at the latest.

   (A) on
   (B) to
   (C) by
   (D) until

2. In order to stay competitive in the computer business, the company invested heavily ------- new technology.

   (A) in
   (B) to
   (C) with
   (D) on

3. Smart Networks claims to be ------- the cutting edge of Internet technology.

   (A) with
   (B) in
   (C) on
   (D) to

4. Mobile Internet technology has had a major impact ------- our lives.

   (A) at
   (B) on
   (C) of
   (D) with

5. Many high-tech companies have built their plants here to take advantage ------- the low cost of land.

   (A) in
   (B) for
   (C) of
   (D) on

6. Technical innovation is instrumental ------- improving the quality of products.

   (A) to
   (B) in
   (C) with
   (D) of

7. I am writing ------- response to your advertisement for a senior
software engineer that appeared on your Web site.

    (A) in
    (B) with
    (C) as
    (D) of

Part 6 解法のコツ 〈定型表現 4〉

手紙やeメールでは、「よろしくお願いいたします」や「お返事をいただければ幸いです」のような
定型表現が数多く登場します。こうした定型表現に慣れておくと、素早く長文を読むことができる
ようになるので、ぜひ慣れておきましょう。

Check

1〜5の英文中で下線を引いた語句とその日本語訳を線で結びましょう。

1. Please find attached our new company •   • よろしくお願いいたします
   brochure.
2. I look forward to hearing from you.   •   • お気軽にお問合せください
3. Thank you for your inquiry.   •   • お問い合わせありがとうございます
4. Thank you in advance.   •   • お返事をいただければ幸いです
5. Please feel free to contact us if you •   • 〜を添付いたします
   have any questions.

Part 6 Text Completion

次の英文を読み、空所に入れるのに最も適切な語句や文を（A）〜（D）から選びましょう。

Questions 8-11 refer to the following e-mail.

From: Olivia Newton <onewton@letsgettogether.com>
To: Gareth Keenan <gkeenan@cmail.com>
Date: September 20th
Subject: Discontinuation of Let's Get Together

Dear All,

Olivia from the Let's Get Together Site here.

Unfortunately, ------- quite a few people are frequently logging into the site, far
fewer are doing so with an active subscription. Over the past year,
subscriptions to the site have paid for the hosting costs, but nothing more.

I have decided to discontinue the security ------- , and from next week the site
will not work with the https:// URL. It will continue to work with the http://
version, however, I will stop updating the site from the end of this month and

it will shortly be discontinued.

For those who have already paid this year's subscription, I will arrange full refunds to the credit cards which ------- to purchase the subscription. If you
10.
no longer use this credit card, please inform me before the end of this month.

------- . I wish you all the best in your future.
11.

Kind regards,
Olivia

8. (A) if
(B) until
(C) although
(D) since

9. (A) concerns
(B) flaw
(C) risk
(D) certificate

10. (A) used
(B) were used
(C) were using
(D) will be used

11. (A) Thank you for your support over the past few years.
(B) We received your comments with much appreciation.
(C) Please find attached our new company brochure.
(D) Please feel free to invite your friends!

Part 7 解法のコツ 〈チャット形式 2〉

オンラインチャットは、基本的に、シングルパッセージ問題の前半に 2 人のやりとりが 1 題、後半に 3 人以上のやりとりが 1 題出題されます。2 人のやりとりは短くて取り組みやすいものが多いですが、3 人以上のやりとりは複雑なので、人物関係を把握するように努めましょう。下の例では、スコットとラジルダのやりとりに途中からネイトが加わっています。呼びかけの言葉に注意して、話の流れを掴みましょう。

オンラインチャットの例

SCOTT (10:12 A.M.) Hi, guys. _____
LAZILDA (10:15 A.M.) _____
SCOTT (10:17 A.M.) _____
LAZILDA (10:20 A.M.) _____
SCOTT (10:22 A.M.) Has anyone made a decision about the platform yet?
LAZILDA (10:27 A.M.) Nate has narrowed it down to a few. Nate, is that right?
NATE (10:35 A.M.) Yes, I've narrowed it down to two candidates, Bazaar and Epigram. I'm favoring the former, but I'd like your input.

_____
_____

ラジルダは「ネイトが 2、3 のプラットフォームに絞り込みました」とスコットに伝え、それからネイトに話しかけています。Nate という呼びかけに注意しましょう。

次の英文を読み、設問に対する答えとして最も適切なものを（A）〜（D）から選びましょう。

Questions 12-15 refer to the following text-message chain.

SCOTT (9:12 A.M.)
Guys, how are preparations going for the webinar?

LAZILDA (9:15 A.M.)
OK, thanks, Scott. The topic's been decided and we have a title. So has the date, but we haven't finalized the exact time. We still need to get a detailed outline and upload it to the registration page.

SCOTT (9:17 A.M.)
Thanks, Lazilda. By registration page, you mean the landing page, right?

LAZILDA (9:20 A.M.)
Right, the main conference site. It has a page for registration.

NATE (9:22 A.M.)
Laz, has anyone made a decision about the platform yet?

LAZILDA (9:27 A.M.)
We've narrowed it down to two candidates, Bazaar and Epigram. I'm favoring the former, but I'd like your input.

SCOTT (9:30 A.M.)
OK, send over the profiles and I'll give you some feedback. How about promotion? Who's taking the lead on that?

NATE (9:35 A.M.)
That'll be me, Scott. I'll be blogging about it, getting it out on the usual channels, Gramsta, Flitter, FaceLink, Talk-Talk, etc.

SCOTT (9:37 A.M.)
FaceLink, Nate? Really?! Does anyone still use that?! Only joking, mate! Good. Sounds like you've got it all covered.

LAZILDA (9:40 A.M.)
The speakers have all given me permission to upload it to BestTube too, so we're good to go on that front.

SCOTT (9:41 A.M.)
Thanks guys. Send over those documents and I'll get back to you.

LAZILDA (9:42 A.M.)
Will do. Catch you later.

12. What is indicated about the webinar?

(A) The date has already been decided.
(B) It is ready for registration.
(C) The topic has yet to be finalized.
(D) Its promotion has just started.

13. According to the chat, who is in charge of promotion?

(A) Lazilda
(B) Scott
(C) Nate
(D) It hasn't been decided.

14. The word "candidates" in paragraph 6, line 1, is closest in meaning to

(A) assets
(B) possibilities
(C) appraisers
(D) positions

15. At 9:37 A.M., what does Scott most likely mean when he writes, "Does anyone still use that"?

(A) He's never heard of FaceLink.
(B) That has already changed its name.
(C) That no longer exists.
(D) He thinks it's not popular anymore.

Communicative Training

Part 7 で取り上げたチャットを使ってパートナーと英語で互いに質問をしてみましょう。答える際は、"Yes." や "No." だけで終わらないよう適宜、情報を追加しましょう。

Student A

Student B（パートナー）に下記の質問をしてみましょう。

Student B

Student A（パートナー）の質問に対して Part 7 の英文を見ながら答えましょう。

1. What does Lazilda say about the topic of the webinar?
2. What does she mean by registration page?
3. Which does she prefer, Bazaar or Epigram?
4. Who is taking the lead on promotion?
5.（You choose!）

本テキストで取り上げている接尾辞一覧

接尾辞とは、specialist の -ist など、語の後ろに付けられる要素を指します。接尾辞を付けることにより品詞が変化することが多く、接尾辞を見ると品詞が推測できます。

名詞を作る接尾辞

接尾辞	意味		例
-ant	人	～する人	applicant（応募者）（< apply）
-ee		～される人	interviewee（受験者）（< interview）
-er		～する人	interviewer（面接官）（< interview）
-ian		～する人	magician（手品師）（< magic）
-ist		～な人、～する人	specialist（専門家）（< special）
-or		～する人	educator（教育者）（< educate）
-ance	こと、状態		compliance（遵守）（< comply）
-ence			existence（存在）（< exist）
-ency			emergency（緊急事態）（< emerge）
-ion, -sion, -tion			invention（発明）（< invent）
-ity, -ty			security（安全）（< secure）
-ment			excitement（興奮）（< excite）
-ness			politeness（礼儀正しさ）（< polite）

動詞を作る接尾辞

接尾辞	意味	例
-ate*	～にする	originate（始まる）（< origin）
-en		widen（～を広くする）（< wide）
-fy, -ify		simplify（単純化する）（< simple）
-ize		specialize（専門にする）（< special）

＊必ずしも動詞とは限らず、fortunate（幸運な）のように形容詞を作る場合もあるので注意が必要。

形容詞を作る接尾辞

接尾辞	意味	例
-able	～できる	imaginable（想像できる）（< imagine）
-al	～の	additional（追加の）（< addition）
-ed	～された	satisfied（満足した）（< satisfy）
-ent	～な	excellent（極めて優れた）（< excel）
-ful	～に満ちた	careful（注意深い）（< care）
-ic	～に関する	atomic（原子の、原子力の）（< atom）
-ical	～に関する	historical（歴史の）（< history）
-ing	～させるような、～している	exciting（興奮させるような）（< excite）
-ive	～な	active（活動的な）（< act）
-less	～のない	careless（不注意な）（< care）
-ory	～な	obligatory（義務的な）（< obligate）
-ous	～な	dangerous（危険な）（< danger）

副詞を作る接尾辞

接尾辞	意味	例
-ly*	～なように	specially（特別に）（< special）

＊必ずしも副詞とは限らず、weekly（毎週の）のように形容詞を作る場合もあるので注意が必要。

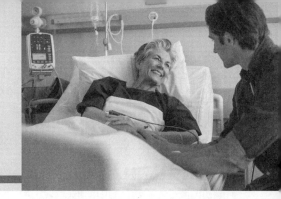

UNIT 09 Health

Vocabulary

1. 1 ～ 10 の語句の意味として適切なものを a ～ j の中から選びましょう。　🎧 2-15

1. symptom	_____	a. 結果
2. chill	_____	b. 手術
3. prevention	_____	c. 疲労
4. anonymous	_____	d. 感染
5. consequence	_____	e. 匿名の
6. physical	_____	f. 寒気、悪寒
7. operation	_____	g. 注射
8. infection	_____	h. 予防
9. exhaustion	_____	i. 身体的な
10. injection	_____	j. 症状

2. 下の接頭辞*に関する表を参考にして、派生語の表を完成させましょう。

接頭辞	意味	例
dis-	～でない (not)	disregard（無視する）(< regard)
in-, im-, il-, ir- *im- は p や m で始まる形容詞、il- は l で始まる形容詞、ir- は r で始まる形容詞の前につくことが多い。		incomplete（不完全な）(< complete) impossible（不可能な）(< possible) illegal（不法の）(< legal) irregular（不規則な）(< regular)
non-		nonprofit（非営利の）(< profit)
un-		unkind（不親切な）(< kind)

単語	逆の意味を持つ単語	単語	逆の意味を持つ単語
comfortable（快適な）	uncomfortable	logical（論理的な）	
stable（安定した）		relevant（関連ある）	
conclusive（決定的な）		toxic（有毒な）	
honest（誠実な）		mature（成熟した）	

接頭辞とは、unable の un- など、語の先頭に付けられて、その語の意味あるいは機能を変える要素を指します。

Part 1 解法のコツ 〈すべての選択肢の確認〉

写真の中で目立つものはキーワードになりやすいですが、多くの場合、複数の選択肢で使われます。最初に聞こえてきたものに飛びつかず、すべての選択肢を確認したうえで解答しましょう。

✌ Check

下の写真の描写として最も適切な英文を 1 〜 4 の中から選びましょう。

1. The doctor is <u>having</u> an injection.
2. The patient is looking at the doctor.
3. The doctor is <u>giving</u> an injection to the patient.
4. The patient is <u>giving himself</u> an injection.

> キーワードは injection ですが、3 つの文に使われており、正答の決め手になるのは下線部です。

Part 1 Photographs

🎧 2-16, 17

(A)〜(D) の英文を聞き、写真を最も適切に描写しているものを選びましょう。

1.

(A)   (B)   (C)   (D)

最初の問いかけに出てきた単語が含まれた選択肢は不正解である場合がほとんどですが、発音が似た単語や同じ発音で意味の異なる単語が入った選択肢も、多くの場合不正解です。

問いかけ	What seems to be the problem?
不正解の応答例	I'm working on a new program.
不正解の応答例	That's a simple mathematical problem.
正解の応答例	I'm having difficulty getting to sleep.

Part 2　Question-Response　　　　　　　　　　　CD 2-18〜22

最初に聞こえてくる英文に対する応答として最も適切なものを (A)〜(C) から選びましょう。

2. Mark your answer.　　(A)　　(B)　　(C)
3. Mark your answer.　　(A)　　(B)　　(C)
4. Mark your answer.　　(A)　　(B)　　(C)
5. Mark your answer.　　(A)　　(B)　　(C)

Part 3　解法のコツ　　〈表現の言いかえ〉

正解の選択肢は、会話の中で使われていた表現をそのまま使うのではなく、別の表現で言いかえた形になっていることがよくあります。下の例では、正解の選択肢は、"Well, I have chills but I don't have a fever." という男性の発言の下線部を feels very cold と言いかえています。選択肢の中に会話で使われていた表現を見つけても、それに飛びつかないようにしましょう。

ex.)

Woman: What seems to be the problem?
Man: 　　Well, I have chills but I don't have a fever.

・ What is the problem with the man?
　(A) He has a fever. 　　　⇒会話で出てきた表現 (fever) はひっかけとして使われています。
　(B) He has a sore throat.
　(C) He has a headache.
　(D) He feels very cold. 　⇒正解は会話内のポイントとなる発言（下線部）を言いかえています！

Part 3　Conversations　　　　　　　　　　　CD 2-23〜25

会話を聞き、6 〜 8 の設問に対する解答として最も適切なものを (A)〜(D) から選びましょう。

6. What does the woman say about the results of the tests?

　(A) They were not available.
　(B) They were worse than she expected.
　(C) They provided no clear diagnosis.
　(D) They were comprehensive.

7. What does the woman say she will do?

　(A) Introduce the man to another doctor
　(B) Carry out a full scan of the man
　(C) Examine the results of the tests
　(D) Conduct the tests again

8. What does the woman suggest the man should do?

(A) Go over his insurance policy with her
(B) Undergo an operation
(C) Purchase a new insurance policy
(D) Check with his insurance company

Part 4 解法のコツ 〈公共放送〉

感染症への対処など、公共性のある情報を告知する公共放送には、下記のような基本的な流れがあります。情報がどのような順序で出てくるか予測することができるので、慣れておきましょう。

1. 挨拶	The following is a public service announcement, brought to you by Radio WABC.
2. 状況	Every year thousands of workers become sick from heat exposure.
3. 追加情報、注意事項	Here are four pieces of advice you should remember when working outdoors.
4. 結び	Thank you for your attention.

Part 4 **Talks**

 2-26〜28

トークを聞き、9 〜 11 の設問に対する解答として最も適切なものを（A)〜(D）から選びましょう。

9. What is this announcement about?

(A) The bad effects of overeating
(B) Human error prevention
(C) The consequences of overworking
(D) Ideal working hours

10. According to the speaker, what leads to poor decision-making?

(A) Excessive eating
(B) Exhaustion
(C) Alcohol abuse
(D) Low self-esteem

11. What does the speaker suggest that the listeners do to learn more?

(A) Use social media
(B) Get a free health consultation
(C) Talk to their colleagues
(D) Visit a Web site

Communicative Training

1. Part 2 のスクリプトにある最初の問いかけを使ってパートナーと英語で互いに質問をして
みましょう。質問に答える際は、下の回答例を参考にしましょう。なお、スクリプトは教
員から配布されます。

Student A
Student B（パート
ナー）に Part 2 の
スクリプトにある最
初の問いかけをして
みましょう。

Student B
Student A（パート
ナー）の質問に対し
て下の回答例を参考
に答えましょう。

Q2
・それは良かったです。
・確かですか？　とても心配です。
・(You choose!)

Q3
・思っていたより良かったです。
・まだ結果を受け取っていません。
・(You choose!)

Q4
・かしこまりました。今日の午後はいかがです
か？
・わかりました。ご希望の日にちはございます
か？
・(You choose!)

Q5
・(それらは) 2、3 日前に始まりました。
・昨日からです。
・(You choose!)

2. Part 3 の対話スクリプトの内容について、パートナーと英語で互いに質問をしてみましょ
う。質問に答える際は、対話スクリプトだけを見るようにし、下の質問は見ないようにし
ましょう。なお、スクリプトは教員から配布されます。

Student A
Student B（パート
ナー）に下記の質問
をしてみましょう。

Student B
Student A（パート
ナー）の質問に対し
て Part 3 の対話ス
クリプトを見ながら
答えましょう。

1. What does the woman say about the results of the man's test?
2. Does she know what is causing his problem?
3. Is she planning to refer him to a specialist?
4. Has he checked with his insurance company yet?
5. (You choose!)

Reading Section

Part 5　解法のコツ　〈接続詞問題〉

接続詞問題の場合、空所前後の単語に着目するのではなく、文全体を読んで内容を理解したうえで解くようにしたほうが良いでしょう。また、while と during など、意味の似通った前置詞との区別が問題になることもあり、その場合は接続詞と前置詞が選択肢に混ざった形になります。なお、接続詞と前置詞を見分けるポイントは次のとおりです。

接続詞	その後に主語と動詞を含む語句（＝**節**）が続きます。 ex.) My father had a heart attack **while** we were having dinner.
前置詞	その後に主語と動詞を含まない語句（＝**句**）が続きます。 ex.) My father had a heart attack **during** dinner.

✌ Check

下線部に注意しながら、1〜4 の英文中のカッコ内から正しい語句を選び○で囲みましょう。

1. Sarah stopped the medication (because / because of) side effects.

2. Leo is fit and well (although / despite) he had a major heart operation six months ago.

3. Rachel was awake (during / while) the operation on her leg.

4. (If / Until) you are interested in receiving free samples of our health care products, fill out the enclosed form.

Part 5　Incomplete Sentences

英文を完成させるのに最も適切な語句を（A）〜（D）から選びましょう。

1. ------- a large donation from an anonymous citizen, the clinic was able to continue its work.

(A) Since
(B) Thanks to
(C) Because
(D) Despite

2. ------- the patient was transferred to this hospital, he had been in St Luke's hospital for a month.

(A) Before
(B) Prior to
(C) After
(D) While

3. ------- the large amount of blood, it was only a minor wound.

(A) Because
(B) Though
(C) Due to
(D) Despite

4. ------- conducting a thorough examination of my legs, my doctor referred me to a knee specialist.

(A) During
(B) Unless
(C) After
(D) As long as

5. Prevention is better than cure, ------- brush your teeth at least twice a day and visit your dentist for regular check-ups.

(A) or
(B) so
(C) because
(D) but

6. ------- walking may be an easy way to exercise, we shouldn't forget that there are many other ways to be active.

(A) Since
(B) Unless
(C) If
(D) While

7. It is often said that the value of health is seldom known ------- it is lost.

(A) until
(B) after
(C) since
(D) though

Part 6　解法のコツ　〈つなぎ言葉 1〉

文脈の理解が必要となる問題では、「したがって」や「しかし」のように、2 つの文をつなぐ副詞（句）を選ばせるものが登場します。これらの副詞（句）は、読解の際に非常に重要ですから確実にマスターしておきましょう。

Check

語群から適切な語句を書き入れ、表を完成させましょう。

結果（したがって、それゆえ）	逆接（しかし、それどころか）	情報追加（さらに、しかも）
		moreover

語群

in addition　　however　　therefore　　✔moreover
besides　　on the contrary　　as a result　　thus

Part 6　Text Completion

次の英文を読み、空所に入れるのに最も適切な語句や文を（A）〜（D）から選びましょう。

Questions 8-11 refer to the following notice.

How to treat a sore throat

The treatment of your sore throat depends on the type of illness: whether your infection is viral or bacterial. In all cases, a consultation with a medical professional is necessary ---8.--- the condition and obtain appropriate treatment. The main symptoms of a sore throat are difficulty swallowing and, sometimes, a high fever. But generally, the ---9.--- is not very long, from 2 to 3

days ------- a week, if you treat it correctly.
          10.

A note of caution
If you have a heart condition such as angina, or even a Covid-19 infection, you should not take anti-inflammatory drugs such as ibuprofen or corticosteroids without medical advice. ------- .
                                                        11.

8. (A) diagnose
    (B) to diagnosing
    (C) diagnosing
    (D) to diagnose

9. (A) duration
    (B) absence
    (C) pause
    (D) wait

10. (A) in
     (B) up to
     (C) by
     (D) on

11. (A) In addition, you need to treat the symptoms.
     (B) For example, there are some natural remedies that can help relieve your symptoms.
     (C) Otherwise you risk making your condition worse.
     (D) However, most sore throats are viral.

| Part 7 | 解法のコツ | 〈記事書式〉 |

新聞や雑誌に掲載された記事は、語数が多く、語彙も難しい傾向にあります。ただし、第 1 段落目に全体の要旨がまとめてあるので、次のような概要に関する問題は第 1 段落をしっかり読めば解くことができます。諦めないようにしましょう。

・What does the article mainly discuss?
・What is the purpose of the article?
・What is the article about?

> いずれも記事の概要を尋ねる設問です。

記事の例

> **Do I need vitamin supplements?**
>
> September 15— _____
> _____
> _____
> _____
> _____
> _____
> _____
> _____
> _____

> 第 1 段落に全体の要旨がまとめてあります。最初に日付が書かれていることもあります。

次の英文を読み、設問に対する答えとして最も適切なものを（A）～（D）から選びましょう。

Questions 12-15 refer to the following article.

There's been a lot of debate recently about supplements. Some health professionals say that most dietary supplements and multivitamins are unnecessary, and that consumers are wasting huge amounts of money buying them. — [1] —. Others—most notably the companies that produce these supplements—disagree, arguing that, for most people, deficiencies in our diets need to be addressed by supplementing essential nutrients.

In many developed countries, up to 50% of the population may be taking some form of multivitamin or supplement, so this is big business, and there's a lot of money at stake. As always, research supporting both sides will be used in evidence. But can those without a financial stake in the game get their voices heard above the powerful lobbying of supplement producers? — [2] —.

The key question in the debate seems to be "Who is taking what?" Pregnant women, for example, have long been recommended to take Omega 3 and folic acid supplements, which are proven to benefit the development of their babies. — [3] —. Another, more surprising outcome is that prisoners who receive vitamin and mineral supplements to their prison diets, show significantly lower rates of violent behavior. — [4] —. This article will investigate this question further and discuss desirable uses of supplements.

12. What does the article mainly discuss?

(A) Rising prices of supplements
(B) A controversy about supplements
(C) Various ways to take supplements
(D) The health hazards that vitamins cause

13. The word "deficiencies" in paragraph 1, line 8, is closest in meaning to

(A) excesses
(B) volumes
(C) shortages
(D) disorders

14. What is NOT indicated about supplements?

(A) Opinions are divided on the necessity of them.
(B) Omega 3 and folic acid supplements help the development of babies.
(C) Some health professionals say that they are unnecessary.
(D) Pregnant women have been recommended not to take them.

15. In which of the positions marked [1], [2], [3], and [4] does the following sentence best belong? "But are supplements essential for everyone?"

(A) [1]
(B) [2]
(C) [3]
(D) [4]

Communicative Training

Part 7 で取り上げた記事を使ってパートナーと英語で互いに質問をしてみましょう。答える際は、"Yes." や "No." だけで終わらないよう適宜、情報を追加しましょう。

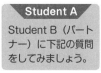

Student A
Student B（パートナー）に下記の質問をしてみましょう。

Student B
Student A（パートナー）の質問に対して Part 7 の英文を見ながら答えましょう。

1. Does this article mainly discuss rising prices of supplements?
2. According to this article, who says that consumers are wasting huge amounts of money buying supplements and multivitamins?
3. What is mentioned as the key question in the debate about supplements?
4. What have pregnant women long been recommended to take?
5.（You choose!）

UNIT 10 Travel

ABCD Vocabulary

1. 1～10の語句の意味として適切なものをa～jの中から選びましょう。　2-29

1. bachelor	_____	a. 貨物運送
2. designated	_____	b. 旅程表
3. reassured	_____	c. 費用、出費
4. reimburse	_____	d. 目的地
5. excursion	_____	e. ～を見渡す、～を見下ろす
6. itinerary	_____	f. 学士
7. destination	_____	g. 指定された
8. expense	_____	h. （払ったお金を）払い戻す、～に返金する
9. overlook	_____	i. 小旅行、遠足
10. freight	_____	j. 安心して

2. 語群の中から適切な日本語訳を選び、派生語の表を完成させましょう。

人を表す名詞を作る主な接尾辞	もとの単語	人を表す名詞
-ant	occupy（　　　）	occupant（　　　）
-ee	examine（試験する）	examinee（　　　）
-er		examiner（　　　）
-ian	civil（市民の、民間の）	civilian（　　　）
-ist	tour（小旅行）	tourist（　　　）
-or	violate（　　　）	violator（　　　）

違反する　　受験者　　占有する　　民間人　　違反者　　占有者　　旅行者　　試験官

Listening Section

Part 1　解法のコツ　〈物の状態〉

〈物〉が中心の写真の場合には、その「位置」と「状態」を確認しましょう。位置関係は、前置詞がポイントになりますが、状態について「一列に並べられている」、「積み重ねられている」などの頻出表現をチェックしておきましょう。

Books are lined up in a row.
（本が一列に並べられています）

Books are stacked in an untidy pile.
（本が無造作に積み重ねられています）

Part 1　Photographs

🎧 2-30, 31

（A）～（D）の英文を聞き、写真を最も適切に描写しているものを選びましょう。

1.

(A)　　(B)　　(C)　　(D)

Part 2 解法のコツ 〈同一単語の繰り返し **2**〉

最初の問いかけに出てきた単語や発音の似た単語が入った選択肢は不正解である場合がほとんどですが、A or B という形式の選択疑問文は例外です。同じ単語が入った選択肢が正解となる場合もあるので注意しましょう。

問いかけ	Should we take a taxi or the train?
正解の応答例	Why don't we take the train?

Part 2 Question-Response

🎧 2-32〜36

最初に聞こえてくる英文に対する応答として最も適切なものを（A）〜（C）から選びましょう。

2. Mark your answer.　　　(A)　　　(B)　　　(C)
3. Mark your answer.　　　(A)　　　(B)　　　(C)
4. Mark your answer.　　　(A)　　　(B)　　　(C)
5. Mark your answer.　　　(A)　　　(B)　　　(C)

Part 3 解法のコツ 〈話者を問う設問〉

話し手の職業を尋ねる設問の場合、選択肢は職業名が並び、短いものが多いので、できるだけ会話を聞く前に選択肢まで見ておくようにしましょう。会話のヒントが得られます。また、"Who most likely is the man?" のようにストレートに職業名を尋ねる質問もあれば、"Where does the man most likely work?" のように勤務先を尋ねる質問もあります。

・Who most likely is the man?
　(A) A travel agent
　(B) A server
　(C) A hotel receptionist
　(D) A bookkeeper

・Where does the man most likely work?
　(A) At a travel agency
　(B) At a restaurant
　(C) At a hotel
　(D) At a conference center

短い選択肢が多いので、できれば事前に目を通しましょう。

Part 3 Conversations

🎧 2-37〜39

会話を聞き、6〜8の設問に対する解答として最も適切なものを（A）〜（D）から選びましょう。

6. Where does the man most likely work?

　(A)　At an airline
　(B)　At a travel agency
　(C)　At a hotel
　(D)　At a freight company

7. What time will the woman arrive at her final destination?

　(A)　4:40 A.M.
　(B)　7:50 A.M.
　(C)　Past 7 P.M.
　(D)　Past 8 P.M.

8. What does the woman mean when she says, "Oh, that's OK"?

(A) She will ask someone else.
(B) She has already checked her airmiles.
(C) She doesn't need an answer from the man.
(D) She has already upgraded her seat.

Part 4 解法のコツ 〈図表問題 **1**〉

Part 3 同様に、Part 4 でも図表付きの問題が出題されます。3 つの設問のうち図表に関するものは
1 つで、"Look at the graphic." という指示が設問の冒頭に書かれています。トークを聞く前に、
図表を見て何が書いてあるのか確認しておきましょう。

プリペイド SIM カードの表だとわかります！

Prepaid SIM Cards

	10GB Plan	13GB Plan	15GB Plan	20GB Plan
Price	$20	$25	$30	$35
Where	SIM Central			Gogo Sims

11. Look at the graphic. What plan does the speaker recommend?
(A) 10GB Plan
(B) 13GB Plan
(C) 15GB Plan
(D) 20GB Plan

Part 4 **Talks**

 2-40〜42

トークを聞き、9 〜 11 の設問に対する解答として最も適切なものを（A）〜（D）から選びましょう。

Prepaid SIM Cards

	10GB Plan	13GB Plan	15GB Plan	20GB Plan
Price	$20	$25	$30	$35
Where	SIM Central			Gogo Sims

9. Why does the speaker call George?

(A) To offer a discount voucher
(B) To provide advice
(C) To check his itinerary
(D) To ask for his advice

10. What does the speaker say about Gogo Sims?

(A) He has a discount coupon.
(B) Its price is reasonable.
(C) It used to be called Sim Central.
(D) It's only available in Terminal 5.

11. Look at the graphic. What plan does the speaker recommend?

(A) 10GB Plan
(B) 13GB Plan
(C) 15GB Plan
(D) 20GB Plan

Communicative Training

1. Part 2のスクリプトにある最初の問いかけを使ってパートナーと英語で互いに質問をしてみましょう。質問に答える際は、下の回答例を参考にしましょう。なお、スクリプトは教員から配布されます。

Student A
Student B（パートナー）に Part 2 のスクリプトにある最初の問いかけをしてみましょう。

Student B
Student A（パートナー）の質問に対して下の回答例を参考に答えましょう。

Q2
・家族旅行で行きました。
・（それは）出張でした。
・(You choose!)

Q3
・もちろん、含んでおります。
・いいえ、宿泊は含まれておりません。
・(You choose!)

Q4
・あなたがしてくれますか？　とても助かります。
・ロブが私たちのためにしてくれました。
・(You choose!)

Q5
・その通りです。（私は）それを楽しみにしています。
・しかし、その日は予定がびっしり詰まっています。
・(You choose!)

2. Part 3の対話スクリプトの内容について、パートナーと英語で互いに質問をしてみましょう。質問に答える際は、対話スクリプトだけを見るようにし、下の質問は見ないようにしましょう。なお、スクリプトは教員から配布されます。

Student A
Student B（パートナー）に下記の質問をしてみましょう。

Student B
Student A（パートナー）の質問に対して Part 3 の対話スクリプトを見ながら答えましょう。

1. According to the man, what time will the woman arrive in Singapore?
2. How long will she have to wait there?
3. Where is her final destination?
4. When will she arrive there?
5. (You choose!)

Reading Section

| Part 5 | 解法のコツ | 〈動詞の形問題3〉 |

動詞の形を問う問題で選択肢に ing 形があった場合、現在分詞と動名詞の2つの可能性があるので注意しましょう。動名詞は、「〜すること」のように動詞を名詞化するものですが、動詞が名詞の働きをするものには to 不定詞もあるので、この2つの使い分けにも慣れておく必要があります。

👉 Check

1〜4の英文中のカッコ内から正しい語句を選び○で囲みましょう。

1. We are currently (seek / seeking) a tour guide and details will be given at interview.
2. The travel agent advised me (to take / taking) out travel insurance.
3. (Reserve / Reserving) airline tickets online saves time and money.
4. I'm considering (to buy / buying) a new suitcase for my next trip abroad.

| Part 5 | Incomplete Sentences |

英文を完成させるのに最も適切な語句を（A）〜（D）から選びましょう。

1. The airline suggests ------- tickets 21 days in advance, so we should do it immediately.

(A) to book
(B) booking
(C) book
(D) booked

2. Standard rooms have a mountain view but no balcony, while Superior rooms have a balcony ------- the pool and garden.

(A) overlook
(B) overlooked
(C) to overlooking
(D) overlooking

3. ------- in the tour is an excursion to the Grand Canyon, which will definitely be the highlight of our trip.

(A) Included
(B) Including
(C) To include
(D) Include

4. Children under two years of age are fully covered by the insurance when ------- with an insured person.

(A) travel
(B) traveled
(C) traveling
(D) to travel

5. Business travel expenses for employees will be ------- based on the actual costs incurred.

(A) reimburse
(B) reimbursed
(C) reimbursing
(D) to reimburse

6. I prefer traveling independently ------- on a package tour, but my wife doesn't.

(A) to go
(B) go
(C) going
(D) to going

7. Excuse me. I'd like ------- a table for three for eight o'clock in the name of Jones.

    (A) to reserve
    (B) reserving
    (C) reserve
    (D) to reserving

Part 6 解法のコツ 〈つなぎ言葉2〉

2つの文をつなぐ副詞（句）では、すでに取り上げた「結果」、「逆接」、「情報追加」に加えて、「例示」、「順序」、「条件」などもよく登場するので、これらについても確認しておきましょう。

Check

語群から適切な語句を書き入れ、表を完成させましょう。

順序（まず、それから、最後に）	例示（例えば）	条件（さもなければ）
	for example	

語群

    finally   ✓for example   otherwise   first   next   for instance   then

---

Part 6 Text Completion

次の英文を読み、空所に入れるのに最も適切な語句や文を（A）〜（D）から選びましょう。

Questions 8-11 refer to the following e-mail.

To: Kathleen Jones <kjones@discovertours.com>
From: Jason Powell <jpowell@cmail.com>
Date: September 28
Subject: Tour Guide Position

Dear Ms. Jones,

I am writing in response to your advertisement for a tour guide that ------- on quickjobsearch.com. I believe I am qualified for this position. As you will see from my attached résumé, my experience and skills match this position's requirements. I have a bachelor's degree ------- tourism and have worked at a travel agency in Springfield for the past five years. I feel confident that with my knowledge and skill, I can make a contribution to your company.

I would appreciate the opportunity to meet with you to discuss my qualifications for ------- position. Please feel free to contact me if you need additional information. ------- .

I look forward to hearing from you.

Sincerely,

Jason Powell

8. (A) appearing
(B) appeared
(C) will appear
(D) have appeared

9. (A) from
(B) for
(C) with
(D) in

10. (A) our
(B) their
(C) your
(D) my

11. (A) I will be happy to supply references upon request.
(B) Thank you for your kind reference letter.
(C) I will keep track of your online job postings and may even reapply.
(D) I am currently seeking employment.

Part 7　解法のコツ　〈トリプルパッセージ問題〉

トリプルパッセージ問題では、クロスレファレンス問題が 5 問中 2 〜 3 問含まれます。1 つの問題を解くのに 3 つの文書 A 〜 C のすべてから情報を組み合わせないといけないことはまれです。1 つの文書を読めば解ける形式、もしくは、文書 B と文書 C のように、2 つの文書に含まれる情報を組み合わせて解く形式になっており、基本的にはダブルパッセージ問題と変わりません。ただし、やはり難しいですので、少しずつ慣れていきましょう。

文書 A（e メール 1）

From: Nancy Lopez
To: All staff
Date: October 19
Subject: New staff member

Dear colleagues,
_____
James will be starting work with us next month.
_____
_____

Nancy

文書 B（e メール 2）

From: Nancy Lopez
To: James Miller
Date: October 19
Subject: Your office

Dear James,
_____
I'd suggest you take the corner office.
_____
_____

Nancy

文書 C（配置図）

	Office 1	Office 2	
Office 3		Office 4	

10. When will James start working?
(A) On October 19
(B) On October 20
(C) In November
(D) In December

> 文書 A の情報が必要です！

11. In the second e-mail, which office does Nancy suggest that James should take?
(A) Office 1
(B) Office 2
(C) Office 3
(D) Office 4

> 文書 B と文書 C の情報が必要です！

次の英文を読み、設問に対する答えとして最も適切なものを（A）～（D）から選びましょう。

Questions 12-16 refer to the following Web page and e-mails.

Welcome to Comfort B&B Web Site

About this space — from your host, Viv

Welcome to BROOK HOUSE in Newtown!

The History and Background

Brook House is a much-loved Newtown landmark. A stunning colonial-era townhouse built in 1760 and fully renovated in 2022, Brook House was home to the son of Edgar Brook, the cotton merchant who built some of Newtown's most beautiful and impressive buildings at the time of the cotton trade boom.

Newtown is fast becoming the most fashionable place to live in the area, and the town center is packed with bars and places to eat. The weekly Cotton Collectibles Market takes place every Saturday and is the ideal place to browse around. Why not time your visit to do some Christmas shopping?

Your home away from home

Your master bedroom has a king-size bed with an ensuite bathroom. The remaining three rooms are furnished with queen-size beds. The main bathroom has a romantic freestanding bath, and you're welcome to cook your own meals in our cool kitchen. The comfortable living room is your home away from home. We hope you enjoy the house as much as we do.

Location & Access

We're right in the center of Newtown, a two-minute walk from downtown eateries and a ten-minute drive from the airport. Special rates are available for large groups. Off-road parking is available for three cars.

Other things to note

We are pet-friendly, but certain restrictions on large pets may apply. Cots and bedding are available. Finally, our beautiful floors will be easily damaged by stiletto heels. We kindly request that you remove all shoes at the door. Slippers are provided.

To:	Viv Feldman <vfeldman@cmail.com>
From:	Stuart Pearson <spearson@cmail.com>
Date:	November 12
Subject:	Two questions

Hi Viv,

I'll be visiting my mother in Newtown, with my wife, 2 sons and 10-month old daughter. We're hoping to make a booking from Tuesday 20th for 7 nights, checking out on the 27th. Before I make the booking, could you kindly confirm the following:

1. You mentioned the availability of a cot for the baby. Is there any extra charge for this?
2. We may have to bring our dog with us. I note that your accommodation is pet-friendly, but is there a designated area for dogs?

Kind regards,

Stuart Pearson

To:	Stuart Pearson <spearson@cmail.com>
From:	Viv Feldman <vfeldman@cmail.com>
Date:	November 13
Subject:	Re: Two questions

Dear Mr. Pearson,

Thank you for your inquiry. Please be reassured that there will be no extra charge. Also, your dog is allowed access to the whole house.

I hope this answers your questions to your satisfaction.

Sincerely,

Viv

12. What is suggested about Edgar Brook?

   (A) He's the current owner of Brook House.
   (B) He was engaged in the cotton trade.
   (C) He started the Cotton Collectibles Market in Newtown.
   (D) He had no children.

13. On the Web page, the word "eateries" in paragraph 4, line 2, is closest in meaning to

   (A) diners
   (B) stores
   (C) bakeries
   (D) offices

14. What is indicated about Brook House?

   (A) Parking space is available for up to two cars.
   (B) Guests are asked to bring their own slippers.
   (C) All bedrooms are furnished with king-size beds.
   (D) Special prices are offered to large groups.

15. According to the first e-mail, how many people will be in Mr. Pearson's party?

   (A) Three
   (B) Four
   (C) Five
   (D) Six

16. What is suggested about Mr. Pearson?

   (A) His grandmother lives in Newtown.
   (B) He's already made a booking for Brook House.
   (C) His daughter's bed will be available free of charge.
   (D) His dog has access only to a designated area of Brook House.

Part 7 で取り上げたウェブページを使ってパートナーと英語で互いに質問をしてみましょう。
答える際は、"Yes." や "No." だけで終わらないよう適宜、情報を追加しましょう。

Student A
Student B（パートナー）に下記の質問をしてみましょう。

Student B
Student A（パートナー）の質問に対して Part 7 の英文を見ながら答えましょう。

1. Who is Edgar Brook?
2. What does the Web page say about Newtown?
3. How many bedrooms does Brook House have?
4. Is Brook House very far from the airport?
5. (You choose!)

UNIT 11 Business

AB CD Vocabulary

1. 1 〜 10 の語句の意味として適切なものを a 〜 j の中から選びましょう。　　　🎧 2-43

1. strategy	_____	a.	承認
2. payroll	_____	b.	再配置、移転
3. acquisition	_____	c.	給与、給与支払簿
4. affiliated	_____	d.	提携している
5. negotiation	_____	e.	株、株式
6. approval	_____	f.	（企業の）吸収合併、買収
7. complaint	_____	g.	一時解雇
8. layoff	_____	h.	戦略
9. share	_____	i.	交渉
10. relocation	_____	j.	苦情

2. 語群の中から適切な語句を選び、会議に関する語句の表を完成させましょう。

会議を招集する	会議の日程を変更する
(　　　　　) a meeting	(　　　　　) a meeting
会議を手配／準備する	**会議に参加する**
(　　　　　) a meeting	(　　　　　) a meeting
会議を中止する	**会議を終わらせる**
(cancel) a meeting	(　　　　　) a meeting
会議を一時休止にする	**会議を延期する**
(　　　　　) a meeting	(　　　　　) a meeting
会議を再開する	**会議を主催する**
(　　　　　) a meeting	(　　　　　) a meeting

✓cancel	attend	host	adjourn	wrap up
reschedule	resume	call	postpone	arrange

119

Listening Section

Part 1   解法のコツ   〈人物（3人以上）の描写 2〉

3人以上の人物が写っている写真の場合、全員の共通点を描写するものが多いですが、特定の人物の動作や服装、持ち物などの描写が正解となる場合もあります。

Check

下の写真の描写として最も適切な英文を 1 〜 4 の中から選びましょう。

1. A woman is writing something on the whiteboard.
2. They're all formally dressed.
3. A man is working on his laptop.
4. They're all looking at the large screen.

Part 1   Photographs   2-44, 45

（A）〜（D）の英文を聞き、写真を最も適切に描写しているものを選びましょう。

1.

(A)   (B)   (C)   (D)

Part 2 解法のコツ 〈間接疑問文〉

"Do you know where he lives?" のように、疑問文を平叙文の語順にして目的語や補語として使うタイプ（間接疑問文）では、途中に出てくる疑問詞が聞き取りのポイントになります。聞き逃さないようにしましょう。

問いかけ	Do you know who's in charge of hiring?
不正解の応答例	Yes, we hired two new employees.
正解の応答例	Mr. Connors in personnel.

Part 2 Question-Response

 2-46〜50

最初に聞こえてくる英文に対する応答として最も適切なものを（A）〜（C）から選びましょう。

2. Mark your answer. (A) (B) (C)
3. Mark your answer. (A) (B) (C)
4. Mark your answer. (A) (B) (C)
5. Mark your answer. (A) (B) (C)

Part 3 解法のコツ 〈場所を問う設問〉

場所に関する設問は会話が行われている場所に関するものが中心ですが、"Where will they meet?" のように話題に関するものが出題されることもあります。いずれの場合も、選択肢は場所の名前で短いものが多いので、できるだけ会話を聞く前に選択肢まで見ておくようにしましょう。会話のヒントが得られます。

- Where most likely are the speakers?
- Where is the conversation taking place?
- Where does the conversation take place?

> いずれも会話の行われている場所を尋ねる設問です。

(A) At a dry cleaner
(B) At a grocery store
(C) At a school
(D) At a hospital

> 短い選択肢が多いのでできれば事前に目を通しましょう。

Part 3 Conversations

2-51〜53

会話を聞き、6〜8の設問に対する解答として最も適切なものを（A）〜（D）から選びましょう。

6. What does the woman suggest doing?
(A) Getting a bank loan
(B) Issuing new shares
(C) Selling shares
(D) Investing in a venture

7. What does the man say he will do?
(A) Invest in the company
(B) Have the lawyer check the regulations
(C) Get the approval of the directors
(D) Go over the regulations and bylaws

8. Where will the man and woman meet tomorrow?

    (A) At the woman's office
    (B) At the man's office
    (C) At the bank
    (D) At the lawyer's office

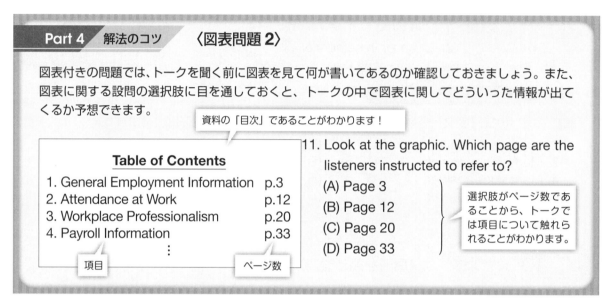

| Part 4 | 解法のコツ | 〈図表問題2〉 |

図表付きの問題では、トークを聞く前に図表を見て何が書いてあるのか確認しておきましょう。また、図表に関する設問の選択肢に目を通しておくと、トークの中で図表に関してどういった情報が出てくるか予想できます。

資料の「目次」であることがわかります！

Table of Contents

1. General Employment Information   p.3
2. Attendance at Work   p.12
3. Workplace Professionalism   p.20
4. Payroll Information   p.33
    ⋮

項目   ページ数

11. Look at the graphic. Which page are the listeners instructed to refer to?

(A) Page 3
(B) Page 12
(C) Page 20
(D) Page 33

選択肢がページ数であることから、トークでは項目について触れられることがわかります。

| Part 4 | Talks |

🎵 CD 2-54～56

トークを聞き、9 ～ 11 の設問に対する解答として最も適切なものを（A）〜（D）から選びましょう。

Table of Contents

1. General Employment Information   p.3
2. Attendance at Work   p.12
3. Workplace Professionalism   p.20
4. Payroll Information   p.33
    ⋮

9. Who is the audience for this talk?

    (A) Job applicants
    (B) Human Resources staff
    (C) New employees
    (D) New managers

10. What does the speaker imply when she says, "You've been at the company only a short while"?

    (A) The listeners are not familiar with the company.
    (B) The listeners haven't received the manual yet.
    (C) The listeners have a lot of energy.
    (D) The listeners must be tired.

11. Look at the graphic. Which page are the listeners instructed to refer to?

    (A) Page 3
    (B) Page 12
    (C) Page 20
    (D) Page 33

Communicative Training

1. Part 2 のスクリプトにある最初の問いかけを使ってパートナーと英語で互いに質問をしてみましょう。質問に答える際は、下の回答例を参考にしましょう。なお、スクリプトは教員から配布されます。

Student A
Student B（パートナー）に Part 2 のスクリプトにある最初の問いかけをしてみましょう。

Student B
Student A（パートナー）の質問に対して下の回答例を参考に答えましょう。

Q2 ・よくわかりません。すみません。 ・まだオフィスにいると思います。 ・(You choose!)	**Q3** ・あと 3 日です。 ・実際、私たちに時間は残されていません。 ・(You choose!)
Q4 ・いいですよ。まっすぐ行って左手にあります。 ・エレベーターの隣です。 ・(You choose!)	**Q5** ・実は、私が担当する予定です。 ・ベンに聞いてもらえませんか？　彼が知っているはずです。 ・(You choose!)

2. Part 3 の対話スクリプトの内容について、パートナーと英語で互いに質問をしてみましょう。質問に答える際は、対話スクリプトだけを見るようにし、下の質問は見ないようにしましょう。なお、スクリプトは教員から配布されます。

Student A
Student B（パートナー）に下記の質問をしてみましょう。

Student B
Student A（パートナー）の質問に対して Part 3 の対話スクリプトを見ながら答えましょう。

1. Does the woman suggest getting a bank loan?
2. Will she find it difficult to get the approval of the directors?
3. Who will check the regulations and bylaws?
4. What does the woman mean when she says, "That shouldn't be a problem"?
5. (You choose!)

Reading Section

Part 5 解法のコツ 〈句動詞問題〉

通常、語彙問題の選択肢は1語ですが、次の例のように2語以上の場合もあります。

The president promised to (run into / look into / put on / give off) the matter.

この場合、〈動詞＋前置詞・副詞〉で特別な意味を持つ句動詞の知識が問われています。上記の問題の場合、「（問題など）を調査する」という意味を持つ look into が正解になります。語彙学習の際には、こうした句動詞にも目を向けましょう。

✓ Check

1～4の英文中で下線を引いた語句とその日本語訳を線で結びましょう。

1. Mr. Boyle asked me to <u>look after</u> the shop while he was out. •　　　　•〜を延期する

2. The bank's reorganization will <u>result in</u> layoffs. •　　　　•〜につながる

3. We cannot <u>put off</u> the meeting any longer. •　　　　•〜を引き継ぐ

4. Anna will <u>take over</u> the job when Peter retires. •　　　　•〜の世話をする

Part 5 Incomplete Sentences

英文を完成させるのに最も適切な語句を（A）～（D）から選びましょう。

1. The toy company is planning to ------- the renovation of its headquarters building.

(A) look down on
(B) move forward with
(C) look up to
(D) get even with

2. Large firms can ------- economies of scale, and we'd have to agree to that.

(A) stay up
(B) burst into
(C) gaze at
(D) benefit from

3. I suggest taking some time to ------- the contract before meeting with your client.

(A) correspond to
(B) refrain from
(C) look over
(D) compensate for

4. The sales assistants are trained to ------- customer complaints in a friendly manner.

(A) deal with
(B) get on
(C) carry on
(D) give in

5. All new employees are required to ------- an orientation session during their first month on the job.

(A) count out
(B) participate in
(C) make up
(D) call on

6. The company has ------- a charitable foundation to improve the lives of children in developing countries.

(A) caught on
(B) filled out
(C) made away
(D) set up

7. At the meeting, the vice president spoke for a long time, but his meaning didn't really ------- .

   (A) come across
   (B) put out
   (C) give off
   (D) count on

Part 6　解法のコツ　〈つなぎ言葉 3〉

Unit 9、10 で 2 つの文をつなぐ主な副詞（句）を確認したので、実際の問題形式で確認してみましょう。結果（したがって）、逆接（しかし）、情報追加（さらに）、例示（例えば）、順序（最初に）のように、パターンが決まっているので、問題演習を繰り返して慣れましょう。

Check

空所に当てはまる語句を語群から選んで、1 ～ 4 の英文を完成させましょう。

1. In order to improve the security of the building, a new security system was installed. (　　　　), extra guards were hired.
2. Living in a flat is all right, but it has its limitations. (　　　　), you don't have your own garden.
3. It's no trouble at all. (　　　　), it will be a great pleasure to help you.
4. Few guitarists can sing as well as they can play. (　　　　), Eric is an exception.

語群

| On the contrary | However | For example | In addition |

Part 6　Text Completion

次の英文を読み、空所に入れるのに最も適切な語句や文を（A）～（D）から選びましょう。

Questions 8-11 refer to the following e-mail.

To:　　　Ian Ure <I.ure@cmail.com>
From:　 Shay Brennan <shayb@bestcapital.com>
Date:　 October 17th
Subject: Relocation of Best Capital

Dear Ian,

Best Capital Ltd. has recently undergone a series of changes in structure and service. A strategy of expansion through acquisition has resulted in our being able to offer improved levels of service to our clients. ------- .
                 8.

Our head office, administration and client services functions have all been relocated to our new facilities in Ireland. Responsibility for these functions passes to Denise Irwin, a very ---9.--- professional in this field, known to many of you personally as the former president of the Keane Investment Group S.A.

Denise ---10.--- non-executive director and will also take responsibility for the day-to-day management of our Fund Advisory Service. We have simplified client contact ---11.--- creating a centralized email address for all day-to-day administrative tasks; please use <admin@bestcapital.com> for all general enquiries.

With kind regards,

Shay Brennan

8. (A) We're not ready to start this process.
   (B) This process is nearing completion and the changes are as follows:
   (C) Thank you for being one of our valued clients.
   (D) It's still uncertain when we can start this process.

9. (A) experiences
   (B) experience
   (C) experiencing
   (D) experienced

10. (A) has been appointed
    (B) has appointed
    (C) will appoint
    (D) is appointing

11. (A) in
    (B) for
    (C) by
    (D) during

Part 7 は全部で 54 問ありますが、1 つの文書（シングルパッセージ）に対して設問が用意されている前半（Questions 147-175）の 29 問と複数の文書（ダブルパッセージ・トリプルパッセージ）に対して設問が用意されている後半（Questions 176-200）の 25 問に分けられます。前半は 1 つの文書に対して設問が 2 〜 4 問されており、比較的短い文書が多いですから短時間で解いていくようにしましょう。また、第 1 問目は下記に示すように文書の目的を問う問題がよく出題されます。

・What is the purpose of the e-mail?
・What is the purpose of the form?
・What is the purpose of the article?
・What is the purpose of the notice?

次の英文を読み、設問に対する答えとして最も適切なものを（A）〜（D）から選びましょう。

Questions 12-15 refer to the following e-mail.

From:	Willie Morgan <wmorgan@topautomotive.com>
To:	Meg Collins <m.collins@cmail.com>
Date:	April 20
Subject:	Registration of your new car

Dear Ms. Collins,

As we informed you the other day, the registration of your new car was successfully completed, and the license plate was issued. Please check the attached vehicle verification data and let me know if you have any questions. You will be able to pick up the car any time from next week, April 24 (Monday). — [1] —.

You may recall that on your last visit, I proposed switching your car insurance to our affiliated policy providers, KPAX Insurance. If you enroll through our company, you will be able to complete all future procedures related to vehicle insurance in coordination with your scheduled car maintenance. — [2] —.

Among the benefits of switching to KPAX are:
1. Quick response in the event of an accident
   We will support you from the moment you report the accident to the insurance company, all the way through the negotiation period after the accident.
2. Highly competitive long-term contracts
   KPAX offers not only single-year contracts but also long-term contracts that offer substantial savings.
3. Coordination with your scheduled car maintenance
   We can inform you about changes in the warranty when you visit us for your scheduled car inspection. — [3] —.

By entrusting us with your automobile insurance, we can provide you with comprehensive, round-the-clock service that enables you to focus on the enjoyment of your new car. — [4] —.

I sincerely hope you could consider KPAX as your preferred vehicle insurer.

With kind regards,

Willie Morgan

12. What is the purpose of the e-mail?

(A) To purchase an insurance policy
(B) To introduce a new insurance company
(C) To advertise new automobile parts
(D) To schedule maintenance work

13. What is indicated about KPAX?

(A) It offers single-year contracts only.
(B) It deals with automobile maintenance services.
(C) It's Ms. Collins' current vehicle insurer.
(D) It's affiliated with Mr. Morgan's company.

14. The word "comprehensive" in paragraph 4, line 2, is closest in meaning to

(A) complete
(B) specific
(C) comfortable
(D) luxurious

15. In which of the positions marked [1], [2], [3], and [4] does the following sentence best belong?
"Our showroom will be open from 9:00 A.M. to 6:00 P.M."

(A) [1]
(B) [2]
(C) [3]
(D) [4]

Communicative Training

Part 7 で取り上げた e メールを使ってパートナーと英語で互いに質問をしてみましょう。答える際は、"Yes." や "No." だけで終わらないよう適宜、情報を追加しましょう。

Student A
Student B（パートナー）に下記の質問をしてみましょう。

Student B
Student A（パートナー）の質問に対して Part 7 の英文を見ながら答えましょう。

1. What did Mr. Morgan attach to the e-mail?
2. When will Ms. Collins be able to pick up her car?
3. What are the opening hours of the showroom?
4. What did he propose to her on her last visit?
5. (You choose!)

UNIT 12 Entertainment

 Vocabulary

1. 1 ～ 10 の語句の意味として適切なものを a ～ j の中から選びましょう。　　2-57

1. applaud	_____		a. 10 年間、10 年	
2. memoir	_____		b. 景品	
3. anticipate	_____		c.（テレビや映画ではなく）じかに、生で	
4. sequel	_____		d. 回顧録	
5. decade	_____		e.（感謝や尊敬の印としての）賛辞、贈り物	
6. look back over	_____		f. ～を一晩考える	
7. sleep on	_____		g. 拍手する、称賛する	
8. tribute	_____		h. ～を振りかえる	
9. in person	_____		i.（物語などの）続編	
10. giveaway	_____		j. ～を予測する、～を見込む	

2. 語群の中から適切な日本語訳を選び、派生語の表を完成させましょう。

名詞を作る主な接尾辞	もとの単語（動詞・形容詞）	名詞
-ence	reside（住む）	residence（　　　　）
-ency	tend（～しがちである）	tendency（　　　　）
-ness	dizzy（目が回って）	dizziness（　　　　）
-ion, -sion, -tion	revise（見直す）	revision（　　　　）
-ment	judge（判断する）	judgment（　　　　）
-ity, -ty	diverse（　　　　）	diversity（　　　　）
-ance	avoid（　　　　）	avoidance（　　　　）

目まい	多様性	回避	傾向	避ける	多様な	住宅	判断	修正

129

Listening Section

| Part 1 | 解法のコツ | 〈種類を表す名詞〉 |

写真に写っている物を描写する際に、具体的な名前を挙げずに種類を表す名詞で表現することがあります。例えば、piano の代わりに musical instrument（楽器）を使う場合などです。こうした種類を表す名詞にも慣れておきましょう。

✌ Check

1～6の語句とその種類を表す語句を線で結びましょう。

1. couch   •   • dairy product
2. coffee   •   • electrical appliance
3. cheese   •   • beverage
4. trousers   •   • clothing
5. vacuum cleaner   •   • vehicle
6. truck   •   • furniture

| Part 1 | Photographs |

 2-58, 59

（A）～（D）の英文を聞き、写真を最も適切に描写しているものを選びましょう。

1.

(A)   (B)   (C)   (D)

問いかけに対して、「どちらでも構わない」、「別の人に聞いてほしい」、「もう少し考えさせてほしい」
のように、あいまいな応答が正解となることもあります。

問いかけ	Would you rather see a movie or watch TV?
正解の応答例	Either is fine with me.

Part 2 　Question-Response

🎧 2-60〜64

最初に聞こえてくる英文に対する応答として最も適切なものを（A）〜（C）から選びましょう。

2. Mark your answer. 　(A) 　(B) 　(C)
3. Mark your answer. 　(A) 　(B) 　(C)
4. Mark your answer. 　(A) 　(B) 　(C)
5. Mark your answer. 　(A) 　(B) 　(C)

Part 3 　解法のコツ　　〈図表問題2〉

図表問題は、会話から得られる情報と図表から得られる情報を組み合わせないと解けない仕組みに
なっています。図表問題の場合、図表にざっと目を通し、どんな情報が載っているのかを会話が流
れてくる前に確認しておきましょう。

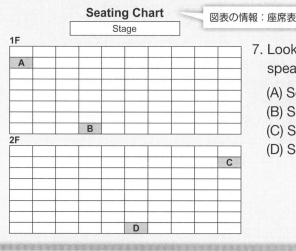

7. Look at the graphic. Where will the speakers sit?

(A) Section A
(B) Section B
(C) Section C
(D) Section D

Part 3 　Conversations

🎧 2-65〜67

会話を聞き、6〜8の設問に対する解答として最も適切なものを（A）〜（D）から選びましょう。

6. What does the man say about the venue?

(A) He performed there a few times.
(B) He's been there a number of times.
(C) He's never been there.
(D) He saw a concert there once.

Seating Chart

Stage

1F

A								
		B						

2F

								C
			D					

7. Look at the graphic. Where will the speakers sit?

(A) Section A
(B) Section B
(C) Section C
(D) Section D

8. What does the man offer to do?

(A) Show the woman where their seats are
(B) Pay for the woman's ticket
(C) Change their seats
(D) Enlarge the seating chart

Part 4 　解法のコツ　〈設問のパターン〉

Part 4 では、1 人の話し手による説明文（トーク）が放送されますので、その話し手の職業や意図などに関する設問がよく出題されます。そのため、設問の中に the speaker（話し手）という表現がよく出てきます。また、話し手が聞き手に何かを提案したり、依頼したりする内容の場合には設問に the listeners（聞き手）がよく使われます。下記に挙げる例で設問のパターンに慣れておきましょう。

・Where does the speaker work? ⇒「話し手の職業は何ですか？」
・What does the speaker say he is doing tomorrow?
　　　　　　　⇒「話し手は明日何をすると言っていますか？」
・Why does the speaker say, "We have a big surprise for you"?
　　　　　　　⇒「なぜ話し手は〜と言うのですか？」
・What does the speaker suggest the listeners do?
　　　　　　　⇒「話し手は聞き手に何をすることを提案していますか？」
・What does the speaker ask the listeners to do?
　　　　　　　⇒「話し手は聞き手に何をするよう求めていますか？」

Part 4 　Talks

 2-68〜70

トークを聞き、9 〜 11 の設問に対する解答として最も適切なものを（A）〜（D）から選びましょう。

9. Who most likely is Roy Springfield?

(A) A film director
(B) A musician
(C) A novelist
(D) An actor

10. Where will Roy go after this show?

(A) A library
(B) A movie theater
(C) A book store
(D) A concert hall

11. What does the speaker encourage the listeners to do?

(A) Listen to the entire show
(B) Come to the studio right now
(C) Send questions by e-mail
(D) Get free samples

Communicative Training

1. Part 2 のスクリプトにある最初の問いかけを使ってパートナーと英語で互いに質問をして みましょう。質問に答える際は、下の回答例を参考にしましょう。なお、スクリプトは教 員から配布されます。

Student A
Student B（パート ナー）に Part 2 の スクリプトにある最 初の問いかけをして みましょう。

Student B
Student A（パート ナー）の質問に対し て下の回答例を参考 に答えましょう。

Q2
・あそこですよ。
・まっすぐ行って、角を右に曲がってください。 右手にあります。
・(You choose!)

Q3
・まったくわかりません。
・メンバーたちが食中毒になった*らしいです。
　　　　　　　　　　　　*get food poisoning
・(You choose!)

Q4
・はい、十分楽しみました。
・はい、ダンサーたちは素晴らしいパフォーマ ンスを披露しました。
・(You choose!)

Q5
・もちろん。喜んでお引き受けいたします。
・私は映画祭について記事を書いたことがあり ません。それでも大丈夫ですか？
・(You choose!)

2. Part 3 の対話スクリプトの内容について、パートナーと英語で互いに質問をしてみましょ う。質問に答える際は、対話スクリプトだけを見るようにし、下の質問は見ないようにし ましょう。

Student A
Student B（パート ナー）に下記の質問 をしてみましょう。

Student B
Student A（パート ナー）の質問に対し て Part 3 の対話ス クリプトを見ながら 答えましょう。

1. What band did the man get tickets to see?
2. Where will it be held?
3. Has the man been to the venue before?
4. On what floor are their seats?
5. (You choose!)

Part 5 解法のコツ 〈慣用句問題〉

His recent success in the entertainment business speaks for (him / his / it / itself).

この問題は、選択肢を見ると代名詞問題と言えますが、speak for itself[themselves]（〜は自明の理である、〜はおのずから明らかだ）という慣用句の知識があればすぐに解けます。語彙学習の際は単語だけでなく、こうした慣用句にも注意を払いましょう。

✌ Check

1〜4の英文中で下線を引いた語句とその日本語訳を線で結びましょう。

1. George takes pride in his work as a film director. •   • コツを知っている
2. One day, out of the blue, she announced her retirement. •   • 突然
3. Because she was new, she didn't know the ropes. •   • 偶然
4. I saw a famous actress by chance at the airport. •   • 〜に誇りを持つ

Part 5 Incomplete Sentences

英文を完成させるのに最も適切な語句を（A）〜（D）から選びましょう。

1. The movie didn't do so well at the box office, but I think it's well written in ------- of the plot.

   (A) vicinity
   (B) terms
   (C) reference
   (D) event

2. I'm afraid that no other coupons can be used in ------- with this coupon.

   (A) accordance
   (B) charge
   (C) addition
   (D) conjunction

3. Ms. Fuller has been nominated for the Academy Award as best supporting actress for three years in a ------- and a lot of people anticipate that she'll finally win the Oscar.

   (A) row
   (B) fix
   (C) spot
   (D) mood

4. We didn't have enough time for dinner before the concert, so we had to make ------- with a quick snack.

   (A) up
   (B) away
   (C) do
   (D) believe

5. By all ------- , the band put on a great show.

   (A) odds
   (B) accounts
   (C) aims
   (D) advantages

6. Emma was such a wet ------- at the party that they never invited her again.

   (A) blanket
   (B) cloth
   (C) towel
   (D) rag

7. I will have to take a rain ------- on going to the
concert tomorrow; I have too many chores to do.

(A) cape
(B) warning
(C) check
(D) shower

Part 6 Text Completion

次の英文を読み、空所に入れるのに最も適切な語句や文を（A）～（D）から選びましょう。

Questions 8-11 refer to the following announcement.

El Borracho Comedy Club!

The El Borracho Comedy Club never sleeps! For nightlife lovers, it's a place where members and their guests can meet, relax, and enjoy a drink and a laugh until the early hours of the morning.

Open from Tuesday to Sunday, we're hosting so many stand-up events that El Borracho is fast becoming downtown North Olmsted's prime entertainment ------- ! You can enjoy one-man shows by ------- comics, see new faces taking their first steps on the comedy circuit, or take part in our famous gong show, in which up-and-coming comedians try to impress ------- three judges.
8.   9.   10.

Tonight's featured act …
Our resident troupe, Los Borrachos, four maniacs who have been acclaimed by the public and the press alike, are back with a new show packed with jokes and sketches— ------- .
11.

8. (A) account
   (B) venue
   (C) allowance
   (D) career

9. (A) established
   (B) establish
   (C) establishing
   (D) being established

10. (A) us
    (B) them
    (C) their
    (D) our

11. (A) you'll be laughed at by everyone!
    (B) we'll really miss your jokes.
    (C) laughter and a unique experience guaranteed!
    (D) everyone will shed bitter tears!

Part 7　解法のコツ　〈キーワードに関する設問〉

Part 7 では限られた時間で大量の英文を読まなければならないので、文書を読む前に設問を読んでおき、解答に必要な情報だけを探すつもりで文書を読んでいく必要があります。その際、次に挙げるような設問の場合、A にあたる語句がキーワードになるので、文書を読む際には A を探し、そこに書かれている内容を素早く読み取りましょう。

　　・What is indicated about A?
　　・What is stated about A?
　　・What is true about A?
　　・What is suggested about A?

いずれも A に関して書かれていることを探しましょう！

次の英文を読み、設問に対する答えとして最も適切なものを（A）～（D）から選びましょう。

Questions 12-15 refer to the following reviews.

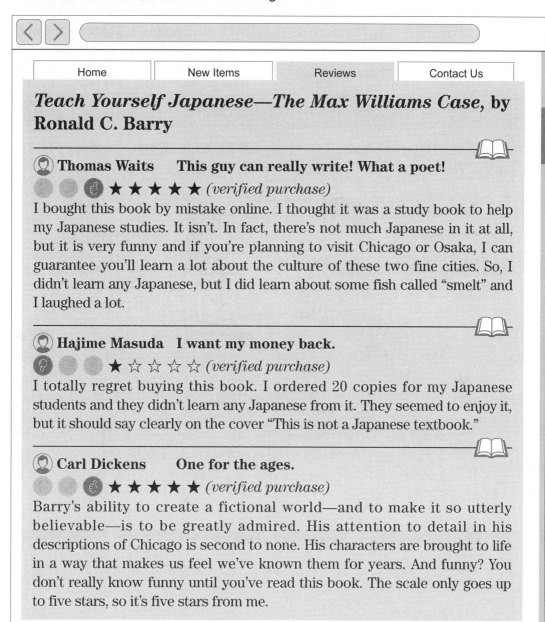

| Home | New Items | Reviews | Contact Us |

Teach Yourself Japanese—The Max Williams Case, by Ronald C. Barry

Thomas Waits   **This guy can really write! What a poet!**
★ ★ ★ ★ ★ *(verified purchase)*

I bought this book by mistake online. I thought it was a study book to help my Japanese studies. It isn't. In fact, there's not much Japanese in it at all, but it is very funny and if you're planning to visit Chicago or Osaka, I can guarantee you'll learn a lot about the culture of these two fine cities. So, I didn't learn any Japanese, but I did learn about some fish called "smelt" and I laughed a lot.

Hajime Masuda   **I want my money back.**
★ ☆ ☆ ☆ ☆ *(verified purchase)*

I totally regret buying this book. I ordered 20 copies for my Japanese students and they didn't learn any Japanese from it. They seemed to enjoy it, but it should say clearly on the cover "This is not a Japanese textbook."

Carl Dickens   **One for the ages.**
★ ★ ★ ★ ★ *(verified purchase)*

Barry's ability to create a fictional world—and to make it so utterly believable—is to be greatly admired. His attention to detail in his descriptions of Chicago is second to none. His characters are brought to life in a way that makes us feel we've known them for years. And funny? You don't really know funny until you've read this book. The scale only goes up to five stars, so it's five stars from me.

12. What is mentioned about Mr. Barry?

(A) He's a language teacher.
(B) His book contains descriptions of Chicago.
(C) He's a nonfiction writer.
(D) He specializes in poetry.

13. The word "verified" in paragraph 1, line 2, is closest in meaning to

(A) confirmed
(B) refuted
(C) recommended
(D) projected

14. What made a customer unhappy?

    (A) The volume of the book
    (B) The ending of the book
    (C) The high price of the book
    (D) The misleading title of the book

15. What does Mr. Dickens discuss in his review?

    (A) His experience in Chicago
    (B) The possibility of a sequel to the book
    (C) The author's attention to detail
    (D) The author's earlier works

Communicative Training

Part 7 で取り上げたレビューを使ってパートナーと英語で互いに質問をしてみましょう。答える際は、"Yes." や "No." だけで終わらないよう適宜、情報を追加しましょう。

Student A
Student B（パートナー）に下記の質問をしてみましょう。

Student B
Student A（パートナー）の質問に対して Part 7 の英文を見ながら答えましょう。

1. Who is the author of *Teach Yourself Japanese—The Max Williams Case*?
2. Is it a language textbook?
3. How does Mr. Masuda feel about buying the book?
4. What made him feel that way?
5. (You choose!)

UNIT 13 Education

ABCD Vocabulary

1. 1～10の語句の意味として適切なものをa～jの中から選びましょう。　🎧 2-71

1. credit	＿＿＿	a. 学期
2. thesis	＿＿＿	b. テーマ
3. registration	＿＿＿	c. 卒業証書、学位記
4. theme	＿＿＿	d. わずらわしい、腹立たしい
5. prerequisite	＿＿＿	e.（科目の）履修単位
6. questionnaire	＿＿＿	f. あらかじめ必要な
7. annoying	＿＿＿	g. アンケート
8. intensive	＿＿＿	h. 履修登録
9. diploma	＿＿＿	i. 卒業論文
10. semester	＿＿＿	j. 集中的な

2. 語群の中から適切な日本語訳を選び、派生語の表を完成させましょう。

動詞を作る接尾辞・接頭辞	もとの単語（名詞・形容詞）	動詞
-ate	active（活動的な）	activate（　　　）
-en	threat（　　　）	threaten（　　　）
-fy, -ify	just（正しい）	justify（　　　）
-ize	agony（　　　）	agonize（　　　）
en-, em-	power（力）	empower（　　　）

脅迫　　苦悩する　　活性化する　　正当化する　　苦痛　　脅す　　力を与える

139

Listening Section

| Part 1 | 解法のコツ | 〈先入観の排除〉 |

写真の中で大きく写っている物にはどうしても注意が向きがちですが、必ずしもそれを描写する文が正解とは限りません。先入観を持たずにすべての文を聞いてから解答しましょう。また、写真に人が写っていても、人が主語となる文が正解とは限らない点も要注意です。

Check

下の写真の描写として最も適切な英文を 1 ～ 4 の中から選びましょう。

1. They're holding their laptops under their arms.
2. The women are staring thoughtfully at the screen.
3. A laptop is being put together.
4. They're gathered to make a toast.

| Part 1 | Photographs | 2-72, 73

（A）～（D）の英文を聞き、写真を最も適切に描写しているものを選びましょう。

1.

(A)   (B)   (C)   (D)

Part 2 解法のコツ 〈主語が異なる応答〉

Wh 疑問文や Yes/No 疑問文が中心になるので、出だしに着目することが重要ですが、主語が何かも確認しておきましょう。"Yes, I did." が正解となるべき質問に対して、"Yes, he did." のように、主語が間違っている選択肢が用意されていることがあります。

問いかけ	Does registration end today?
不正解の応答例	Yes, they do.
正解の応答例	No, we have until tomorrow.

Part 2 Question-Response 　　　　　　　　　　　　 2-74〜78

最初に聞こえてくる英文に対する応答として最も適切なものを（A）〜（C）から選びましょう。

2. Mark your answer.　　　(A)　　　(B)　　　(C)
3. Mark your answer.　　　(A)　　　(B)　　　(C)
4. Mark your answer.　　　(A)　　　(B)　　　(C)
5. Mark your answer.　　　(A)　　　(B)　　　(C)

Part 3 解法のコツ 〈3 人での会話〉

会話は基本的に 2 人ですが、全部で 13 ある会話のうち 2 つ程度は 3 人の会話となっています。その場合、"Questions XX through XX refer to the following conversation with three speakers." という指示文が会話の前に流れ、3 人の会話であることがわかるようになっています。2 人の会話と 3 人の会話で解き方に大きな違いはありませんが、1 人しかいない性別に関する設問が多いので、その人の発言に注意しましょう。また、設問に具体的な人名が出てくることも特徴の 1 つです。

　ex.) 男性 2 名、女性 1 名の会話における設問例

　・Who is the woman?　　⇒ 1 名しか登場しない性別に関する設問が目立つ！

　・What is indicated about Charlie?

　　　　　　　　　　⇒同じ性別が複数いるため、人名が記載されることが多い！

Part 3 Conversations 　　　　　　　　　　　　 2-79〜81

会話を聞き、6 〜 8 の設問に対する解答として最も適切なものを（A）〜（D）から選びましょう。

6. What are the speakers talking about?

(A) Their theses
(B) Their grades
(C) Their registration
(D) Their examination schedule

7. What does the woman say she wants to do?

(A) Earn as many credits as possible
(B) Go on to graduate school
(C) Decide on the theme of her thesis soon
(D) Keep one day free for her thesis

141

8. What is indicated about Charlie?

(A) He has already chosen the courses to take.
(B) He has decided on the theme of his thesis.
(C) He wishes to be more organized.
(D) He has already completed online registration.

Part 4 解法のコツ 〈学内アナウンス〉

学内アナウンスには、下記のような基本的な流れがあるので、情報がどのような順序で出てくるか
予測することができます。慣れておきましょう。

1. 呼びかけ	Attention all students taking Professor Brown's Intercultural Communication course. ⇒対象は異文化間コミュニケーションの受講生	
2. 目的	Due to a technical problem in room 202, today's lecture will be held in the auditorium in Building 1. ⇒教室の変更連絡	
3. 追加情報	Considering the travel time to the auditorium, the lecture will begin at 4:30, not at 4:20. ⇒開始時間の変更連絡	
4. 結び	We apologize for any inconvenience this may cause.	

Part 4 Talks

2-82〜84

トークを聞き、9〜11 の設問に対する解答として最も適切なものを（A）〜（D）から選びましょう。

9. Who is this announcement directed to?

(A) Freshmen
(B) Sophomores
(C) Juniors
(D) Seniors

10. According to the speaker, what time will Professor Holder's lecture start?

(A) At 5:00 P.M.
(B) At 5:30 P.M.
(C) At 6:00 P.M.
(D) At 6:30 P.M.

11. According to the speaker, what is indicated about Slade Hall?

(A) It is located in Building 3.
(B) The employment advisory seminar will be held there today.
(C) Professor Holder's lecture was previously scheduled to be held there.
(D) It is temporarily closed today.

Communicative Training

1. Part 2のスクリプトにある最初の問いかけを使ってパートナーと英語で互いに質問をして みましょう。質問に答える際は、下の回答例を参考にしましょう。なお、スクリプトは教 員から配布されます。

Student A
Student B（パート ナー）に Part 2 の スクリプトにある最 初の問いかけをして みましょう。

Student B
Student A（パート ナー）の質問に対し て下の回答例を参考 に答えましょう。

Q2
・はい、アメリカに留学したいと考えています。
・いいえ、興味がありません。
・(You choose!)

Q3
・8 つの授業に登録しました。
・まだしていません。あなたはいくつの授業に 登録しましたか？
・(You choose!)

Q4
・えっ、本当ですか？　仕事を探しているのか と思っていました。
・知っています。彼女は一生懸命勉強してい ます。
・(You choose!)

Q5
・3 時半だと思います。
・よくわかりません。ウェブサイトで確認した らどうですか？
・(You choose!)

2. Part 3 の対話スクリプトの内容について、パートナーと英語で互いに質問をしてみましょ う。質問に答える際は、対話スクリプトだけを見るようにし、下の質問は見ないようにし ましょう。

Student A
Student B（パート ナー）に下記の質問 をしてみましょう。

Student B
Student A（パート ナー）の質問に対し て Part 3 の対話ス クリプトを見ながら 答えましょう。

1. Are the speakers talking about their examinations?
2. What does the woman want to keep one day completely free for?
3. Has Charlie chosen the courses to take yet?
4. What is he waiting for?
5. (You choose!)

Reading Section

Part 5　解法のコツ　〈代名詞問題 2〉

代名詞問題には、人称代名詞の他に関係代名詞も含まれます。関係代名詞の問題の場合は、まず空所の前を見て、先行詞にあたる名詞（句）が人であるか、それとも人以外であるかを確認します。次に、空所の後の部分がどのような構造になっているかを見極めましょう。

また、下の図を参考にして主な関係代名詞について確認しておきましょう。

先行詞	主格	所有格	目的格
人	who	whose	who / whom
人以外	which	whose	which
人・人以外	that	−	that

> 目的格の関係代名詞は省略されることもあります。

 Check

下線部に注意して、1〜4の英文中のカッコ内から正しい語を選び○で囲みましょう。

1. Applicants (who / whose / which) passed the written tests were called for an interview.
2. (What / That / Which) I do now has nothing to do with my major at university.
3. This course is designed for students (who / whose / which) first language is not English.
4. Kevin's daughter got accepted at the college (who / that / he) went to 30 years ago.

Part 5　**Incomplete Sentences**

英文を完成させるのに最も適切な語句を（A)〜(D）から選びましょう。

1. I really appreciate your invitation to give a lecture at your university, but I'll be out of town on business in early June, ------- makes it impossible to accommodate your proposed schedule.

   (A) which
   (B) who
   (C) what
   (D) that

2. We don't know the person ------- donated this money to our school.

   (A) which
   (B) whose
   (C) who
   (D) what

3. Emma's academic ability is evidenced by the annual Award for Academic Excellence ------- she received from our university.

   (A) who
   (B) what
   (C) whose
   (D) that

4. This school is especially for children ------- schooling has been disrupted by illness.

   (A) who
   (B) whose
   (C) whom
   (D) their

5. No one in the classroom made any sense of ------- Professor Brown was referring to.

- (A) what
- (B) that
- (C) which
- (D) whose

6. Goodsentences.com is an online sentence dictionary site, ------- you can find good example sentences for a large number of words.

- (A) on which
- (B) that
- (C) whose
- (D) which

7. This intensive course is designed for those ------- have little or no teaching experience in science.

- (A) what
- (B) whose
- (C) which
- (D) who

Part 6 解法のコツ 〈コロンとセミコロン〉

英語の句読点のうち、コロン（:）とセミコロン（;）は形が似ており、使い方も紛らわしいものです。コロンやセミコロン自体について出題されるわけではありませんが、用法を理解しておくと、その後にどのような情報が続くかを理解しやすくなります。下記の表で確認しておきましょう。

記号	主な用法
コロン（:）	「すなわち」の意味を持っており、その後に、具体的な例や引用、補足説明などが続きます。 1. 例示 　There are three types of muscle in the body: cardiac, smooth, and skeletal. 　（体内の筋肉には3つの種類があります。心筋、平滑筋、骨格筋です） 2. 補足説明 　Bill is my ideal partner: smart and highly competent. 　（ビルは私の理想のパートナーです。頭が良くて非常に有能です）
セミコロン（;）	関係のある2つの文をつなぎますが、下記の2つのパターンがあります。 1. and や so などの接続詞の代わりに用いて、2つの文をつなぎます。 　I was exhausted; I went straight to bed. 　（私はひどく疲れていました。それですぐに寝ました） 　= I was exhausted, so I went straight to bed. 　× I was exhausted; I usually skip breakfast. 　　　　関連のない2つの文はセミコロンでつなげられません。 2. however や therefore などの接続副詞と共に用いて2つの文をつなぎます。 　I had planned to go out with my friends; however, I was too tired. 　（友人と出かける予定にしていました。しかし、疲れすぎていました） 　= I had planned to go out with my friends. However, I was too tired. 　= I had planned to go out with my friends, but I was too tired. 　× I had planned to go out with my friends, however I was too tired.

次の英文を読み、空所に入れるのに最も適切な語句や文を（A）～（D）から選びましょう。

Questions 8-11 refer to the following announcement.

Free Online Urdu Classes!

Course Requirements: Intended for anyone wishing to study Urdu, ideally with an interest in Pakistani culture or planning to live or work in Pakistan. There is no prerequisite level; ------- .
8.

Objectives: The first objective will be to learn to read and write, ------- will allow you to follow all the other courses. The open course ------- four main
9.   10.
categories: learning to read and write, vocabulary, grammar, and everyday conversation. The course will provide you with 20 expertly written downloadable PDFs and by the end of this program, you will have learned 500+ vocabulary words and phrases, acquired basic Urdu grammar and conjugation, learned to count in Urdu, and have the ability to read basic Urdu script.

For more information and ------- , click here.
11.

---

8. (A) this course is designed for those who have learned Urdu.
(B) you are required to complete a beginner's course first.
(C) you need to have enough ability to communicate freely in Urdu.
(D) even absolute beginners can follow these courses.

9. (A) which
(B) that
(C) they
(D) who

10. (A) consists
(B) comprises
(C) concludes
(D) concedes

11. (A) register
(B) registered
(C) to register
(D) will register

Part 7 の後半の 25 問（Questions 176-200）は複数文書問題となっており、読まなければいけない英文の量が一気に増えます。また、その中でもクロスレファレンス問題は複数の文書に書かれた内容を組み合わせないと解けませんので難易度が高いと言えます。しかし、複数文書問題で出題される 5 問のすべてがクロスレファレンス問題というわけではなく、5 問中 1～2 問に限られています。また、4 問目以降に配置されていることがほとんどですから、まずは 1 つの文書内の情報で解くことができる問題を済ませ、余裕を持ってクロスレファレンス問題に取り掛かりましょう。なお、クロスレファレンス問題を解く際に英文を最初から読み直していると時間が足りなくなってしまいます。問題に関係する箇所のみに目を通すだけに留めましょう。

次の英文を読み、設問に対する答えとして最も適切なものを（A）～（D）から選びましょう。

Questions 12-16 refer to the following e-mail and form.

To:	Jennifer Schmidt <jschmidt@cmail.com>
From:	Thomas Miller <tmiller@astratc.edu>
Date:	January 10
Subject:	Please take a moment to rate today's seminar.

Dear Ms. Schmidt,

Thank you for attending our live online seminar "Developing effective facilitating skills" today.

I'd like to find out what you thought of it via a short questionnaire. In return, I'm happy to send you a summary of the seminar with extra tips and examples you can use for your class.

Please access the following URL and fill out the questionnaire. It will not take more than five minutes.
www.astrateachingcollege.edu/onlineseminar/survey

Thanks again, and I hope to see you next time.

Sincerely,

Thomas Miller
Astra Teaching College
www.astrateachingcollege.edu

Participant Satisfaction Questionnaire

Thank you for taking the time to fill out this participant satisfaction questionnaire. It should take less than five minutes of your time. Click the "Submit" button to submit the questionnaire. Please rate your satisfaction level with each of the following statements:

1: Very dissatisfied   2: Somewhat dissatisfied
3: Neither satisfied or dissatisfied   4: Somewhat satisfied   5: Very satisfied

	1	2	3	4	5
1. How satisfied are you with the theme?	☐	☐	☐	☐	☑
2. How satisfied are you with the content?	☐	☐	☐	☐	☑
3. How satisfied are you with the length?	☐	☐	☑	☐	☐
4. How satisfied are you with the delivery?	☐	☑	☐	☐	☐
5. Rate your overall satisfaction of the seminar.	☐	☐	☐	☑	☐

Comments (optional)

I've been teaching at high school for 15 years, but I didn't know much about the difference between facilitation and traditional teaching. So, I found the theme of the seminar very interesting and useful. In fact, today's online session provided me with comprehensive knowledge about effective facilitation, and I'd like to try some of the facilitating skills that I learned. I should note, however, that somehow the sound cut out several times during the seminar, which was really annoying. Overall, I enjoyed the seminar very much and I'm looking forward to receiving the material you offered for answering the questionnaire.

Sincerely,

Jennifer Schmidt

Submit

12. What is the purpose of the e-mail?

   (A) To answer a questionnaire
   (B) To ask for feedback
   (C) To extend an invitation to a seminar
   (D) To provide a summary of the seminar

13. According to the form, what aspect of the seminar did Ms. Schmidt rate the lowest?

   (A) The theme
   (B) The content
   (C) The length
   (D) The delivery

14. In the form, the word "facilitation" in paragraph 2, line 2, is closest in meaning to

   (A) support
   (B) treatment
   (C) relationship
   (D) method

15. What is suggested about Ms. Schmidt?

   (A) She's fresh out of college.
   (B) She's looking for a career change.
   (C) She's an experienced teacher.
   (D) She's a specialist on facilitation.

16. What does Ms. Schmidt say she is looking forward to receiving?

(A) A brochure
(B) An invitation to the next seminar
(C) A summary of the seminar
(D) Results of the questionnaire

Communicative Training

Part 7 で取り上げたアンケート用紙を使ってパートナーと英語で互いに質問をしてみましょう。答える際は、"Yes." や "No." だけで終わらないよう適宜、情報を追加しましょう。

Student A
Student B（パートナー）に下記の質問をしてみましょう。

Student B
Student A（パートナー）の質問に対して Part 7 の英文を見ながら答えましょう。

1. What does Jennifer Schmidt do?
2. Did she feel the seminar was interesting and useful?
3. Was she satisfied with the delivery of the seminar?
4. What made her feel that way?
5. (You choose!)

主な接頭辞一覧

　接頭辞とは、unable の un- など、語の先頭に付けられて、その語の意味あるいは機能を変える要素を指します。例えば、un- は通常、語の意味を逆にしますので、「(〜することが) できる」という意味の able に対して unable は「(〜することが) できない」という意味を表します。接尾辞同様、接頭辞の知識があると、未知の単語の意味をある程度推測できます。

接頭辞	意味	例
bi-	2 つの (two)	biweekly (隔週の) (< weekly)
dis-	〜でない (not)	disregard (無視する) (< regard)
in-, im-, il-, ir- ＊ im- は p や m で始まる形容詞、il- は l で始まる形容詞、ir- は r で始まる形容詞の前につくことが多い。	〜でない (not)	incomplete (不完全な) (< complete) impossible (不可能な) (< possible) illegal (不法の) (< legal) irregular (不規則な) (< regular)
mono-	1 つの (one)	monocultural (単一文化の) (< cultural)
multi-	多くの (many)	multicultural (多文化の) (< cultural)
non-	〜でない (not)	nonprofit (非営利の) (< profit)
out-	外の (outside) 〜以上に (bigger, better, longer, etc.)	outpatient (外来患者) (< patient) outlive (〜より長生きする) (< live)
post-	後の (after)	post-tax (〈収入が〉税引き後の) (< tax)
pre-	前に (before)	pre-tax (〈収入が〉税引き前の) (< tax)
re-	再び (again)	rearrange (再配置する) (< arrange)
semi-	半分 (half)	semi-automated (半自動の) (< automated)
un-	〜でない (not) 元に戻して (back)	unkind (不親切な) (< kind) undo (元に戻す) (<do)

pre- 前の (before)
prewar (戦前の)

post- 後の (after)
postwar (戦後の)

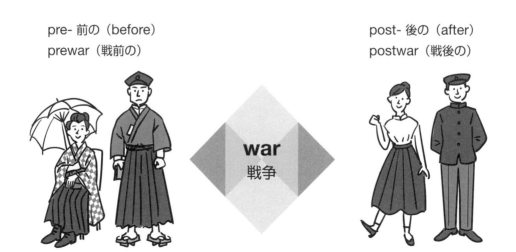

war
戦争

UNIT 14 Housing

AB CD Vocabulary

1．1 ～ 10 の語句の意味として適切なものを a ～ j の中から選びましょう。　CD 2-85

1. prospective	＿＿＿＿	a．査定、評価
2. ownership	＿＿＿＿	b．（道路から自宅車庫までの）私道
3. landlord	＿＿＿＿	c．家主、大家
4. criterion	＿＿＿＿	d．（判断の）基準、尺度
5. liability	＿＿＿＿	e．賃借人
6. tenant	＿＿＿＿	f．法的責任
7. authentic	＿＿＿＿	g．所有権
8. renew	＿＿＿＿	h．本物の、真正の
9. driveway	＿＿＿＿	i．有望な、見込みのなる
10. assessment	＿＿＿＿	j．～を更新する

2．語群の中から適切な日本語訳を選び、派生語の表を完成させましょう。

形容詞を作る主な接尾辞	もとの単語（名詞・動詞）	形容詞
-able	vary（変わる）	variable（　　　　）
-al	triumph（　　　　）	triumphal（勝利の）
-ed	assure（　　　　）	assured（保証されて）
-ent	insist（主張する）	insistent（　　　　）
-ful	waste（無駄、無駄にする）	wasteful（　　　　）
-ic	icon（偶像）	iconic（　　　　）
-ical	type（種類・型）	typical（　　　　）
-ing	inspire（奮い立たせる）	inspiring（　　　　）
-ive	aggress（　　　　）	aggressive（攻撃的な）
-less	flaw（　　　　）	flawless（完璧な）

無駄の多い	執拗な	奮い立たせるような	保証する	勝利
攻撃を仕掛ける	欠点	典型的な	変わりやすい	象徴的な

Part 1 解法のコツ 〈受動態〉

物が中心の写真の場合、その状態を描写するのに受動態が多く使われます。「(物は)〜されている最中だ」という現在進行形の受動態も出題されるので、〈is/are + being + 過去分詞〉の部分を聞き逃さないようにしましょう。

Computers are placed on desks.
(パソコンが机に設置されています) [状態]

An electric car is being charged.
(電気自動車は充電中です) [動作]

Part 1 Photographs

2-86, 87

(A)〜(D) の英文を聞き、写真を最も適切に描写しているものを選びましょう。

1.

(A)　　(B)　　(C)　　(D)

問いかけに対して、「誰から聞いたのですか？」のように、質問で返す応答が正解となる場合があります。自然なやりとりになるように、最初の問いかけから対話の場面を想像することが大切です。

| 問いかけ | You moved to a new apartment, didn't you? |
| 正解の応答例 | Who told you that? |

Part 2　Question-Response　🎧 2-88〜92

最初に聞こえてくる英文に対する応答として最も適切なものを（A）〜（C）から選びましょう。

2. Mark your answer.　　(A)　　　(B)　　　(C)
3. Mark your answer.　　(A)　　　(B)　　　(C)
4. Mark your answer.　　(A)　　　(B)　　　(C)
5. Mark your answer.　　(A)　　　(B)　　　(C)

Part 3　解法のコツ　〈定番の設問〉

会話の話題や場所、話し手の職業など、毎回出題される定番の設問があるので、設問を見たらすぐにわかるように慣れておきましょう。

- What most likely is the man?　　⇒男性の職業がポイント！
- Where is the conversation taking place?　⇒会話が行われている場所がポイント！
- What does the woman suggest?　　⇒女性が提案している内容がポイント！
- What does the woman suggest the man do?
  　　　　　　　　　　　　　　⇒女性が男性に提案している内容がポイント！
- What will the man offer to do?　　⇒男性が申し出ている内容がポイント！

Part 3　Conversations　🎧 2-93〜95

会話を聞き、6 〜 8 の設問に対する解答として最も適切なものを（A）〜（D）から選びましょう。

Floor Plan

	Room 3 occupied	Room 4 unoccupied
Room 2 unoccupied		
	Room 1 occupied	

▲Stairs

6. Look at the graphic. Which room does the woman decide to take?

(A) Room 1
(B) Room 2
(C) Room 3
(D) Room 4

7. What is indicated about the room the woman has decided to take?

(A) It overlooks the garden.
(B) It is cooler in summer.
(C) It has the best view.
(D) It gets more sunlight.

8. What does the man offer to do?

(A) Help the woman find a roommate
(B) Let the woman see the room
(C) Introduce the woman to the landlord
(D) Show the garden to the woman

住宅に関連した対話では、不動産業者と顧客との売買や賃貸借に関するものの他、住宅に関するトラブルに関するものなどがよく出題されます。すでに取り上げた plumber（配管工、水道業者）の他、トピックに関連した頻出用語を確認しておきましょう。

Check

1～6の語句とその日本語訳とを線で結びましょう。

1. poor ventilation	•	• 電気配線の誤接続
2. clogged drains	•	• 水漏れ
3. faulty electrical wiring •		• 排水管の詰まり
4. roof damage	•	• カビの増殖
5. water leakage	•	• 換気不良
6. mold growth	•	• 屋根の損傷

Part 4　**Talks**　　　　　　2-96～98

トークを聞き、9～11の設問に対する解答として最も適切なものを（A）～（D）から選びましょう。

9. Who most likely is Mr. McMurphy?

(A) A building superintendent
(B) A cleaner
(C) A real estate agent
(D) A resident of apartment 53

10. According to the speaker, what is the problem?

(A) Roof damage
(B) Water leakage
(C) Poor ventilation
(D) Faulty electrical wiring

11. What is indicated about Ms. Torrance's apartment?

(A) The ceiling has fallen in on her.
(B) The electricity is off.
(C) The toilet won't flush.
(D) Her carpet is seriously damaged.

Communicative Training

1. Part 2 のスクリプトにある最初の問いかけを使ってパートナーと英語で互いに質問をしてみましょう。質問に答える際は、下の回答例を参考にしましょう。なお、スクリプトは教員から配布されます。

Student A
Student B（パートナー）に Part 2 のスクリプトにある最初の問いかけをしてみましょう。

Student B
Student A（パートナー）の質問に対して下の回答例を参考に答えましょう。

Q2
・とても快適で気に入っています。
・まあまあです（文句は言えません）。
・(You choose!)

Q3
・絶対、家具付きのほうです。
・どちらでもいいです。気にしません。
・(You choose!)

Q4
・月に 800 ドルです。
・月に 1,000 ドル以上です。
・(You choose!)

Q5
・広くてとても素敵ですね。
・家賃がとても高いような気がします。
・(You choose!)

---

2. Part 3 の対話スクリプトの内容について、パートナーと英語で互いに質問をしてみましょう。質問に答える際は、対話スクリプトだけを見るようにし、下の質問は見ないようにしましょう。なお、スクリプトは教員から配布されます。

Student A
Student B（パートナー）に下記の質問をしてみましょう。

Student B
Student A（パートナー）の質問に対して Part 3 の対話スクリプトを見ながら答えましょう。

1. How many vacant rooms are there in this shared apartment?
2. Which room overlooks the garden, the larger or the smaller one?
3. How much less expensive is the smaller room?
4. What does the woman mean when she says, "I guess that decides it"?
5. (You choose!)

Part 5　解法のコツ　〈動詞の形問題 4〉

動詞の形を問う問題には、「(人) に〜させる」という意味を表す使役動詞の用法が出題されることがあります。have、let、make はいずれも≪使役動詞＋目的語＋動詞の原形≫というパターンで使われますが、get だけは動詞の原形ではなく to 不定詞が使われますので注意が必要です。

Check

1 ～ 4 の英文中のカッコ内から正しい語句を選び○で囲みましょう。

1. Russell lets me (stay / to stay) at his apartment whenever I want.
2. The real estate agent tried to get Lily (sell / to sell) her house, but she wouldn't.
3. I'll have to have the plumber (fix / fixed) the leak.
4. We had our house (renovate / renovated) recently, so now it's a two-family house.

Part 5　Incomplete Sentences

英文を完成させるのに最も適切な語句を（A)～（D) から選びましょう。

1. We were made ------- half an hour before the real estate agent prepared the contract.

(A) wait
(B) waited
(C) to wait
(D) to waiting

2. If we really want this housing project ------- , we'll have to put more effort into it.

(A) succeed
(B) to succeed
(C) succeeding
(D) to succeeded

3. Last month's water bill was much higher than usual, so we had our house ------- for water leaks.

(A) inspect
(B) to inspect
(C) inspecting
(D) inspected

4. I'm not going to have my apartment lease ------- even if the landlord offers to lower the rent.

(A) renew
(B) renewed
(C) renewing
(D) to renew

5. The real estate agent would like you to let him ------- when you plan to sign the contract.

(A) to know
(B) known
(C) know
(D) knew

6. Mr. Benning often said that he liked his house very much, so we don't know what caused him ------- it.

(A) to sell
(B) sell
(C) sold
(D) selling

7. We are planning to have the small bedroom
------- into a second bathroom.

(A) convert
(B) to convert
(C) converting
(D) converted

語句挿入問題では、Part 5 同様に前置詞問題がありますが、as for（〜に関しては）のような群前置詞が選択肢に並ぶことも多くあります。群前置詞とは、2 語以上の単語がつながって、1 つの前置詞のように使われる表現ですが、because of（〜のために）など、頻出のものは確実にチェックしておきましょう。

✌ Check

1 〜 5 の英文中で下線を引いた語句とその日本語訳を線で結びましょう。

1. As of May 1, we have not received the shipment. •   • 〜のお返しに
2. The will was made two days prior to his death. •   • 〜を代表して
3. On behalf of the department I would like to thank you all. •   • 〜の前に
4. I am writing with regard to your letter of March 15. •   • 〜に関して
5. Can I buy you lunch in return for your help? •   • 〜の時点で

| Part 6 | Text Completion |

次の英文を読み、空所に入れるのに最も適切な語句や文を（A）〜（D）から選びましょう。

Questions 8-11 refer to the following announcement.

Shared rental apartments with FLATMATE!

Need a room in a shared house? Have a room that needs a tenant? FLATMATE! offers you a new vision of cohabitation that takes the stress out of the search and ------- the barriers associated with finding someone to share accommodation. With FLATMATE! cotenants no longer get together solely for financial reasons but also to share, support and help each other.
_{8.}

Meeting new people, deepening friendships, or simply sharing your skills and expertise in return for a place to live— ------- . Together it's better! ------- you're a senior retiree, a young professional, a single-parent or divorcee, a family or a couple, there's a place for everyone, and we can find ------- in four easy steps:
1. Register with FLATMATE!
2. Create your own authentic, personalized profile.

3. Browse our selection of rental profiles and match your criteria to our cotenants.

4. Submit a proposal to your preferred accommodation.

8. (A) removal
(B) removing
(C) removed
(D) removes

9. (A) all these things can contribute to our well-being and quality of life.
(B) it's time for you to start your new career!
(C) they have changed your life all of a sudden.
(D) in addition, we are very pleased to offer you a new accommodation.

10. (A) Once
(B) Because
(C) Whether
(D) Unless

11. (A) you
(B) yours
(C) yourself
(D) your

Part 7 解法のコツ 〈**NOT** 型設問〉

Part 7 は限られた時間で大量の英文を読む必要があるので時間との戦いになります。その中でも特に時間がかかるのが、「～でないものはどれですか？」というタイプの設問です。選択肢（A）～（D）のそれぞれについて文書の中に記載があるかどうかを確認していかなければならないので、どうしても解答に時間がかかります。実際の試験の場合にはこうした設問は後回しにするなどして時間を有効に活用しましょう。

設問例

・What is NOT true about A?

・What is NOT mentioned as a feature of A?

・What does NOT apply to A?

時間がない時は「～でないもの」タイプの設問は後回しにするのも１つの手段です！

Part 7 Reading Comprehension

次の英文を読み、設問に対する答えとして最も適切なものを（A）～（D）から選びましょう。

Questions 12-15 refer to the following Web page.

Home Central

| Home | For Sale | Access | Contact Us |

New on the market!

A lovely 1930's brick-built detached one-story house, beautifully presented both inside and out. With three bedrooms and a large open-plan living/dining room, this property is well located, close to the town center and convenient for rail and bus transport.

This property has recently been extensively renovated. In addition to its hall, large open-plan living/dining room, modern fitted kitchen, one single and two double bedrooms, it boasts a brand-new bathroom, a utility room and a fresh air ventilation system.

Set away from the road, there is a large driveway leading to the 2-car garage, with additional off-road parking. This property's spacious and expertly maintained garden is another stand-out feature. Patio space includes a barbecue pit and outdoor pizza oven. The south-facing garden enjoys afternoon and evening sun, ideal for relaxation and small parties.

 Disclaimer—Terms of Use & Limitations of Liability
Home Central will assume no responsibility for the accuracy of the information on the Web site. Our employees have no authority to offer any assurances with regard to the ownership of listed properties.

Online Home Value Assessments
Online home value assessments provide sellers with an estimate for their asking price and should not be considered as an official property appraisal or market analysis. Estimates arising from online home value assessments should be independently verified by prospective buyers.

---

12. What type of business is Home Central?

(A) An investment company
(B) A real estate company
(C) A housing finance company
(D) A home building company

13. The word "assurances" in paragraph 4, line 4, is closest in meaning to

(A) denials
(B) rewards
(C) values
(D) guarantees

14. What is NOT indicated about the property advertised on the Web page?

(A) Home Central will be responsible for the correctness of the information.
(B) Its spacious garden is maintained by experts.
(C) It is conveniently located in terms of public transportation.
(D) It is a single-story house with three bedrooms.

15. What will online home value assessments provide to sellers?

    (A) An official property appraisal
    (B) An official market analysis
    (C) A quotation
    (D) A list of prospective buyers

Communicative Training

Part 7 で取り上げたウェブページを使ってパートナーと英語で互いに質問をしてみましょう。
答える際は、"Yes." や "No." だけで終わらないよう適宜、情報を追加しましょう。

Student A
Student B（パートナー）に下記の質問をしてみましょう。

Student B
Student A（パートナー）の質問に対して Part 7 の英文を見ながら答えましょう。

1. How many stories does the property advertised on the Web page have?
2. Is it located far away from the town center?
3. Has it been renovated?
4. Does Home Central assume responsibility for the accuracy of the information on the Web site?
5. (You choose!)

巻末資料

航空機（の利用）に関連した重要語句一覧

departure　出発

語句	意味
airline	航空会社
airplane ticket	航空券
boarding pass	搭乗券
passport	パスポート
check-in counter	チェックインカウンター
check-in baggage	預け入れ荷物
carry-on baggage	機内持ち込み手荷物
excess baggage	超過手荷物
security check	保安検査（場）
connecting flight counter	乗り継ぎカウンター

arrival　到着

語句	意味
landing card	入国カード
immigration	入国管理（所）
customs	税関
customs declaration form	税関申告書
baggage claim area	手荷物受取所
destination	目的地
domestic flight	国内便
international flight	国際便
direct flight	直行便
connecting flight	乗継便

本テキストで取り上げている接尾辞一覧

名詞を作る接尾辞

接尾辞	意味		例
-ant	人	～する人	applicant（応募者）（< apply）
-ee		～される人	interviewee（受験者）（< interview）
-er		～する人	interviewer（面接官）（< interview）
-ian		～する人	magician（手品師）（< magic）
-ist		～な人、～する人	specialist（専門家）（< special）
-or		～する人	educator（教育者）（< educate）
-ance	こと、状態		compliance（遵守）（< comply）
-ence			existence（存在）（< exist）
-ency			emergency（緊急事態）（< emerge）
-ion, -sion, -tion			invention（発明）（< invent）
-ity, -ty			security（安全）（< secure）
-ment			excitement（興奮）（< excite）
-ness			politeness（礼儀正しさ）（< polite）

動詞を作る接尾辞

接尾辞	意味	例
-ate*	～にする	originate（始まる）（< origin）
-en		widen（～を広くする）（< wide）
-fy, -ify		simplify（単純化する）（< simple）
-ize		specialize（専門にする）（< special）

＊必ずしも動詞とは限らず、fortunate（幸運な）のように形容詞を作る場合もあるので注意が必要。

形容詞を作る接尾辞

接尾辞	意味	例
-able	～できる	imaginable（想像できる）（< imagine）
-al	～の	additional（追加の）（< addition）
-ed	～された	satisfied（満足した）（< satisfy）
-ent	～な	excellent（極めて優れた）（< excel）
-ful	～に満ちた	careful（注意深い）（< care）
-ic	～に関する	atomic（原子の、原子力の）（< atom）
-ical	～に関する	historical（歴史の）（< history）
-ing	～させるような、～している	exciting（興奮させるような）（< excite）

接尾辞	意味	例
-ive	〜な	active（活動的な）（< act）
-less	〜のない	careless（不注意な）（< care）
-ory	〜な	obligatory（義務的な）（< obligate）
-ous	〜な	dangerous（危険な）（< danger）

副詞を作る接尾辞

接尾辞	意味	例
-ly*	〜なように	specially（特別に）（< special）

＊必ずしも副詞とは限らず、weekly（毎週の）のように形容詞を作る場合もあるので注意が必要。

主な接頭辞一覧

接頭辞	意味	例
bi-	2つの（two）	biweekly（隔週の）（< weekly）
dis-	〜でない（not）	disregard（無視する）（< regard）
in-, im-, il-, ir- ＊im- は p や m で始まる形容詞、il- は l で始まる形容詞、ir- は r で始まる形容詞の前につくことが多い。	〜でない（not）	incomplete（不完全な）（< complete） impossible（不可能な）（< possible） illegal（不法の）（< legal） irregular（不規則な）（< regular）
mono-	1つの（one）	monocultural（単一文化の）（< cultural）
multi-	多くの（many）	multicultural（多文化の）（< cultural）
non-	〜でない（not）	nonprofit（非営利の）（< profit）
out-	外の（outside） 〜以上に（bigger, better, longer, etc.）	outpatient（外来患者）（< patient） outlive（〜より長生きする）（< live）
post-	後の（after）	post-tax（〈収入が〉税引き後の）（< tax）
pre-	前に（before）	pre-tax（〈収入が〉税引き前の）（< tax）
re-	再び（again）	rearrange（再配置する）（< arrange）
semi-	半分（half）	semi-automated（半自動の）（< automated）
un-	〜でない（not） 元に戻して（back）	unkind（不親切な）（< kind） undo（元に戻す）（<do）

TEXT PRODUCTION STAFF

edited by	編集
Minako Hagiwara	萩原 美奈子
Takashi Kudo	工藤 隆志

| cover design by | 表紙デザイン |
| Nobuyoshi Fujino | 藤野 伸芳 |

| illustration by | イラスト |
| Yoko Sekine | 関根 庸子 |

CD PRODUCTION STAFF

narrated by	吹き込み者
Jack Merluzzi (AmE)	ジャック・マルージ (アメリカ英語)
Rachel Walzer (AmE)	レイチェル・ワルザー (アメリカ英語)
Guy Perryman (BrE)	ガイ・ペリマン (イギリス英語)
Sarah Greaves (AsE)	セーラ・グリブズ (オーストラリア英語)
Neil DeMaere (CnE)	ニール・デマル (カナダ英語)

A COMMUNICATIVE APPROACH TO
THE TOEIC® L&R TEST Book 3: Advanced
コミュニケーションスキルが身に付く
TOEIC® L&R TEST《上級編》

2024年1月20日　初版発行
2024年2月15日　第2刷発行

著　者	角山 照彦　Simon Capper
発行者	佐野 英一郎
発行所	株式会社 成美堂
	〒101-0052　東京都千代田区神田小川町3-22
	TEL 03-3291-2261　FAX 03-3293-5490
	https://www.seibido.co.jp

印刷・製本　三美印刷株式会社

ISBN 978-4-7919-7291-3　　　　　　Printed in Japan